12.60

Ingram

3/11/21

The

PACIFIC CREST TRAIL

THE

PACIFIC

CREST

TRAIL

A VISUAL

COMPENDIUM

JOSHUA M. POWELL

SASQUATCH BOOKS
SEATTLE

Printed in China

SASQUATCH BOOKS with colophon is a registered trademark of Penguin Random House LLC

25 24 23 22 21   9 8 7 6 5 4 3 2 1

Editor: Jen Worick
Production editor: Jill Saginario
Art director: Anna Goldstein
Production designer: Alison Keefe
Designer: Joshua M. Powell

Library of Congress Cataloging-in-Publication Data
Names: Powell, Joshua M., author.
Title: The Pacific Crest Trail : a visual compendium / Joshua M. Powell.
Description: Seattle, WA : Sasquatch Books, 2021. | Includes index.
Identifiers: LCCN 2020018224 (print) | LCCN 2020018225 (ebook) | ISBN
   9781632173287 (paperback) | ISBN 9781632173294 (ebook)
Subjects: LCSH: Pacific Crest Trail--Description and travel. | Pacific
   Crest Trail--Pictorial works. | Hiking--Pacific Crest Trail. | Powell,
   Joshua M.--Travel--Pacific Crest Trail.
Classification: LCC GV199.42.P3 P68 2021 (print) | LCC GV199.42.P3
   (ebook) | DDC 917.9043--dc23
LC record available at https://lccn.loc.gov/2020018224
LC ebook record available at https://lccn.loc.gov/2020018225

ISBN: 978-1-63217-328-7

Sasquatch Books
1904 Third Avenue, Suite 710
Seattle, WA 98101

SasquatchBooks.com

Yes sir, yes madam, I entreat you. Get out of those motorized wheelchairs, get off your foam rubber backsides, stand up straight like men! Like women! Like human beings! And walk— *walk*—WALK upon our sweet and blessed land!

Edward Abbey, *Desert Solitaire*

Traveling in these giant cedar canoes, the Haida would regularly paddle their home into, and out of, existence. With each collective paddle stroke they would have seen their islands sinking steadily into the sea while distant snow-covered peaks scrolled up before them like a new planet. Few people alive today have any notion of how it might feel to pull worlds up from beyond the horizon by faith and muscle alone.

John Vaillant, *The Golden Spruce*

Nearly every American hungers to move.

John Steinbeck, *Travels with Charley*

CONTENTS

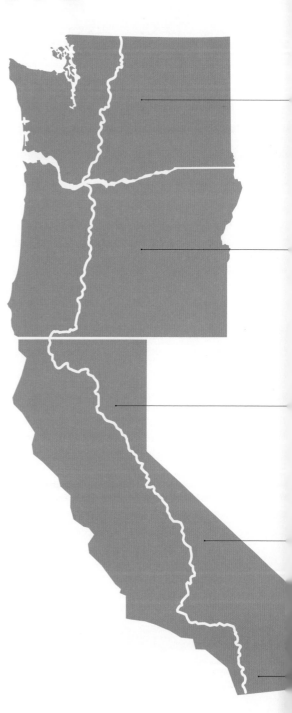

Introduction

SOMEWHERE IN THE Glacier Peak Wilderness I recorded in my journal the following thoughts:

> I'm excited about creating a PCT book and feel like I need to make it happen. No matter how hard it is or how long it takes. I've got to be as committed to it as I have been to hiking the trail itself.

I made it a goal to create a book about the Pacific Crest Trail at nearly the same time I decided to walk from Mexico to Canada. I had been working as a bookseller and a book designer and other than hiking, books were the main focus of my life. It only made sense to combine the two passions.

It turns out that creating this book has proven more difficult than walking to Canada, though no less enjoyable. Throughout the experience I often thought what a gift it was to continually relive my time on the trail and that even if the book was never published, the process alone was more than worth it. It's surprising for me to consider that the PCT has been a consistent focus of my life for nearly a decade.

I committed to thru-hiking in the fall of 2012 as I stood along the trail in the Goat Rocks Wilderness in Southern Washington. I stared out at the Knife's Edge and Mount Rainier, one of the most iconic views of the PCT, and made a pact with myself to return to that point, having walked there from Mexico. It was a gorgeous October day, part of a wonderful backpacking trip during that Indian Summer. I had met several thru-hikers on the trip—at the "ass end" of their cohort, as they put it. Summer ended soon enough and some of them made it to Canada and some did not. One of them, in fact, ended up spending a week lost in the snow north of Stevens Pass and was lucky to survive.

I made it back to that point in 2014, but the only thing I saw was the silhouettes of my thru-hiking companions as they disappeared into the fog ahead of me. The previous day had brought the worst rain of

Steinbeck

About halfway through California I found a copy of John Steinbeck's *Cannery Row* and decided for the first time to carry a book with me on the trail. I chose it for the fact that I enjoyed Steinbeck, but perhaps just as much for the fact that it was a small and lightweight paperback. I read in the long evening light of summer and was surprised to soon discover that the protagonist of *Cannery Row*, based on Steinbeck's friend Ed Ricketts, was none other than a long-distance hiker, before such a notion existed. This novel has become strongly linked to my experience on the PCT and thus I can't help but consider Steinbeck's Monterey as much of a PCT trail town as Lone Pine, Ashland, or Stehekin. After the trail I read and reread many of Steinbeck's books, as well as his biography, and found a surprising number of connections between his writing and my time on the trail. I've included some of these observations in this book.

my entire thru-hike, leaving the beautiful scenery of the Goat Rocks to my memory and replacing it with the cold, wet discomfort of life on the trail. It was one of many difficult days I experienced over the course of that summer. When my hike was over, however, I often claimed that I never had a bad day on the trail. Bad minutes and bad hours, sure, but never a bad day.

It was Washington that always kept me going. Had I never moved to Washington I may never have become a backpacker and would surely never have hiked the PCT. I came to know the beauty of the Cascades, and knowing what lay ahead gave me motivation to walk back home as I progressed step by step across California and Oregon. So, when I crossed the Columbia River and set foot in Washington, I set foot in the state where I fell in love with hiking. It is where I gradually found myself taking longer and longer day hikes, until eventually I mustered the courage to embark on my first overnight trip in the shadow of the tallest of all the Cascadian volcanoes—Mount Rainier. The state where I first set foot on the PCT and stared south, wondering what it would feel like to have walked all the way from Mexico, imagining the terrain I would pass through along the way and how beautiful it might be. The state where I would weather a hailstorm in a high alpine basin, grabbing my tarp just before it blew away and then holding it firmly against the ground on both sides, fists clenched and digging into the earth as I waited an hour for the storm to pass. Where I experienced the joy of solitude in true wilderness, far from any road. Where I forded a remote backcountry creek nearly a hundred miles from the ocean, filled with salmon floating in its current like glinting jewels—their crimson backs reflecting the sun like rubies. And though I did not know it at the time, when I crossed that bridge over the Columbia, it was where I would fall in love in an altogether different way. I had already met my future wife on an August afternoon amidst the High Divide of the Olympic Mountains. Washington was my home before the trail and over the course of the summer, the PCT had become a new home and the two became entwined.

THIS BOOK HAS been created from a northbound thru-hiker's perspective and from the perspective of someone who hiked the trail in 2014. It was that year, two years after the publication of *Wild* by Cheryl

Trail Name

Hiking up into the foothills of the San Bernardinos, I climbed through a narrow canyon as daylight seeped from the sky and the mountains became enveloped in darkness. In the distance behind me I saw several pricks of light amidst the pitch black—the headlamps of other hikers. A moment later I was startled by a bright light moving directly toward me on the trail. It was another thru-hiker who had dropped his sunglasses a few yards south. He retrieved them and then caught back up with me, introducing himself, appropriately, as Lost and Found. We hiked together through the dark hills until we finally reached a remote preserve and trout farm that allows hikers to camp on their property. We paused at a trail register to sign our names and I jokingly complained about how hard it is for a left-handed person to write in a three-ring binder.
"I think you've got yourself a trail name now," he said. "You're Southpaw."

When I Introduced Myself on the Trail
28% of people knew what Southpaw meant
72% of people looked at me with a blank stare

Strayed, that the PCT was really on its way to becoming a popular trail. If you are thru-hiking in 2021, your experience will be much different than mine, just as my experience may sound vastly different to someone who hiked the trail in 2007.

My experience is also that of a white male. All thru-hikers worry about the heat, lack of water, or inclement weather. There are, however, a great number of worries that I was unburdened by during my hike. Worries that a woman or person of color carries with them on the trail. Worries that may surface when they meet a stranger, hitchhike, or enter an unfamiliar town. When I walked past a Confederate flag in Sierra City, California, I took offense, yet continued on feeling safe and unthreatened.

There are significant historical and systemic reasons why people of color have been unable to establish a tradition of outdoor recreation, while Indigenous people have been forcibly removed from their land to create national parks and wilderness. As I recall, I met very few people of color on my entire thru-hike. It is important that the trail community grow to reflect our greater society. To that end, let us all seek out and promote the stories of those who are not in the majority.

I HOPE THIS BOOK inspires people to hike the PCT, whether for a day or an entire summer, but as the trail becomes increasingly crowded, it is imperative to preserve it for those who will feel inspired to hike it years down the road. Respect the trail towns you visit and the people who call them home. Be a good ambassador for the trail. While hiking, leave those Sharpies in your pocket and refrain from writing on signs. Take only photos and leave behind the flowers, bird feathers, and animal bones for others to enjoy. Respect wildlife and forgo building a campfire. Bury your waste properly and pack out your toilet paper. Camp only in established sites. I regret falling short of these rules on a few occasions during my hike. I encourage you to educate yourself and follow Leave No Trace ethics. If not, we risk loving this trail to death.

Joshua M. Powell, "Southpaw"

Playing in the woods as a child in Virginia
1980s–1990s

Occasional hikes in the Appalachians during college
1999–2004

Driving out West, visiting national parks and doing short day hikes
2004

Day hiking in Japan
2005–2007

Move to Seattle, day hiking in the Cascades
2008–2009

Taking longer and longer day hikes and setting foot on the PCT for the first time
2009–2010

Finally doing my first overnight backpack in Mount Rainier National Park
2010

Backpacking as much as possible for the next three summers, taking my first weeklong backpacking trip on the Wonderland Trail around Mount Rainier
2010–2013

Hiking the PCT
2014

495
MILES

Washington

456
MILES

Oregon

540
MILES

Northern California

457
MILES

Central California

702
MILES

Southern California

PART ONE

The PCT — AT A — GLANCE

April 24 to September 2

132
TOTAL DAYS

2,653.3
TOTAL MILES HIKED

25.1
**MILES PER DAY
AVERAGED**

35.2
**MOST MILES HIKED
IN A SINGLE DAY**

9
ZERO DAYS

484,422'
TOTAL ELEVATION GAIN

483,408'
TOTAL ELEVATION LOSS

MOST ENJOYABLE SECTION
Stevens Pass to Stehekin in Washington

LEAST ENJOYABLE SECTION
McArthur-Burney Falls State Park to the
McCloud River in Northern California

ROAD CROSSINGS
8 interstates
35 highways
67 paved roads
133 unpaved roads

HIGHEST POINT
Forester Pass | 13,153'

LOWEST POINT
Columbia River | 0'

5,394
TOTAL PHOTOS

5,065
**SCENERY
PHOTOS**

38.4
**PHOTOS PER
DAY AVERAGED**

1.9
**PHOTOS PER
MILE AVERAGED**

36
SHOWERS IN 132 DAYS

19
NIGHTS CAMPED ALONE

17
BLISTERS

107
SONGS STUCK IN MY HEAD

11
MOST DAYS WITHOUT A SHOWER

27
MOST MILES IN A DRY STRETCH WITHOUT A WATER CACHE

3
BEARS SEEN

8
LOST BALLOONS FOUND IN THE BACKCOUNTRY

FAVORITE TOPONYM OF THE PCT
Inconsolable Range

MOST COMMON WAY PEOPLE MISTAKENLY REFER TO THE PACIFIC CREST TRAIL
Pacific "Coast" Trail

MY TWO GREATEST FEARS
- Getting an overuse injury that ends my hike
- Giving up

SUN
—
112 DAYS

RAIN
—
19 DAYS

WIND
—
23 DAYS

CLOUDS
—
22 DAYS

THUNDER-STORMS
—
5 DAYS

FOG
—
6 DAYS

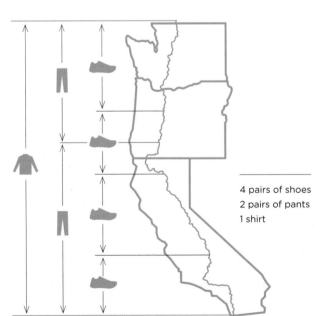

4 pairs of shoes
2 pairs of pants
1 shirt

Thru-Hiking Glossary

Backcountry Primitive areas in nature where development is limited to trails, unpaved roads, and ranger stations.

Base weight The weight of everything a hiker carries, minus consumables such as water, food, or fuel.

Blowdown A tree that has been uprooted or broken by the wind, causing it to fall across the trail and hinder a hiker's progress.

Cathole A hole dug at least six inches deep in which to bury one's waste. Catholes should be dug a reasonable distance from the trail, campsites, or water sources. Toilet paper should typically be packed out, especially in drier areas where it does not easily decompose.

Cowboy camp To sleep under the stars, rather than inside a tent or under a tarp. This typically requires only a ground sheet, sleeping pad, and sleeping bag.

Dry camping Camping at a site where there is no adjacent water source.

Flip flop Hiking a trail out of order rather than in one continuous direction. For example, hiking Southern California, then skipping ahead to Northern California to avoid the Sierras in a high snow year. In this scenario the Sierras would be returned to later in the season when the snow has melted.

The herd The large group of hikers that typically forms during the beginning of a long-distance trail due to similar starting times, naturally dissipating as the season progresses. The herd can also result from "bottlenecking" due to hiker events, trail angel homes, or delays due to snow or inclement weather.

Hiker box A container of some sort where hikers can discard unwanted gear or food, leaving it for others.

Hike your own hike A phrase indicating that there are a multitude of ways to approach a long-distance hike and that one should be accepting of another hiker's differing approach, so long as it does not detract from anyone else's experience.

Leave no trace A method of spending time on the trail with the least amount of impact. Examples include packing out all trash, not contaminating water sources, burying waste properly, respecting wildlife, and not camping in fragile areas.

Nero A day in which a hiker covers only a few miles, typically when hiking into or out of a trail town.

NoBo A northbound thru-hiker.

Postholing Sinking knee deep into soft snow. Typically occurs when descending a mountain pass in the afternoon. It significantly slows travel and is dangerous due to the potential for striking one's leg against a hidden boulder.

Skip Intentionally not hiking a portion of the trail with no intention of returning to it later.

Slackpack Hiking a section of trail without heavy gear such as a shelter or sleeping bag. This typically involves outside support, such as another person shuttling the hiker and/or gear.

SoBo A southbound thru-hiker.

Stealth camp To secretly camp in an unestablished site in the backcountry or on private land without permission.

Thru-hike To hike the entire length of a long-distance trail in one attempt.

Trail register A log found along the trail or in trail towns in which hikers can sign their names and leave comments or notes for other hikers.

Trail angel Anyone who helps a hiker by giving them a ride, providing food or drink, or offering them a place to relax, clean up, or stay the night. Anyone who helps build and maintain the trail is an angel as well.

Trail magic Acts of kindness or support offered to hikers, typically in the form of water caches, cold drinks, or food.

Trail name A nickname given to a thru-hiker during his or her hike. Thru-hikers typically adopt a trail name rather than using their real name.

Trail town Small towns either directly on the trail or in close vicinity (reached by road walking, side trails, or hitchhiking) where hikers can resupply, eat at restaurants, bathe, and sleep under a roof.

Water cache Containers of water left for hikers along the trail, typically at road crossings.

Wilderness A subset of the backcountry where development is limited only to hiking trails. No roads, mechanized equipment, or vehicles are permitted.

Yogi Receiving free refreshments or rides by ingratiating yourself to non-thru-hikers (as in Yogi the Bear).

Yo-yo Hiking a long-distance trail from one end to the other, then turning around and hiking back to the original starting point, essentially hiking the trail twice in one attempt. An endeavor reserved solely for the insane.

Zero day A day in which no miles are hiked, typically spent in a trail town.

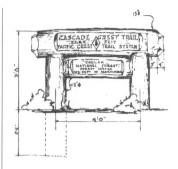

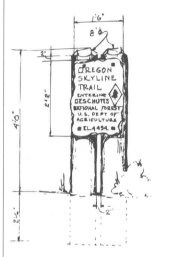

Building Blocks of the Pacific Crest Trail

The first known proposal for a trail spanning California, Oregon, and Washington was made in 1926 by Catherine Montgomery. In 1968 the PCT was designated a national scenic trail and was officially completed in 1993. The PCT was composed of four already existing trails:

Cascade Crest Trail | WA ▬▬▬

Skyline Trail | OR ▬▬▬

Tahoe-Yosemite Trail | CA ▬▬▬

John Muir Trail | CA ▬▬▬

Cascade Crest Trail signs can still be found at several points in Washington:

Glacier Peak Wilderness
Snoqualmie Pass
White Pass
Goat Rocks Wilderness

Original 1937 Forest Service diagrams of Cascade Crest Trail and Oregon Skyline Trail signs.

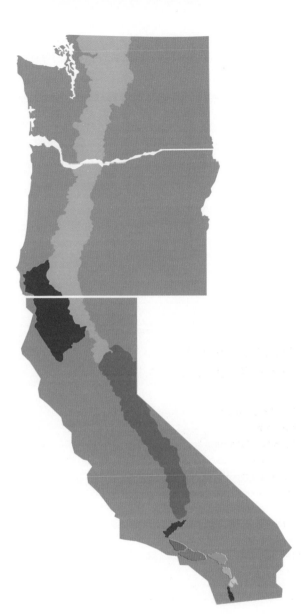

Cascades

Klamaths

Cascades

Sierra Nevada

Tehachapis
Sierra Pelonas
San Gabriels
San Bernardinos   **Transverse Ranges**
San Jacintos
Santa Rosas
Lagunas   **Peninsular Ranges**

Mountain
Ranges
of the
Pacific Crest Trail

Ecoregions of the Pacific Crest Trail

North Cascades, 1
Cascades, 2
Klamath Mountains and California High North Coast Range, 3
Eastern Cascades Slopes and Foothills, 4
Sierra Nevada, 5
Mojave Basin and Range, 6
Southern California Mountains, 7
Southern California and Northern Baja Coast, 8

West Coast Ecoregions Adjacent to the PCT
Coast Range, 9
Puget Lowland, 10
Willamette Valley, 11
Columbia Plateau, 12
Columbia Mountains, 13
Blue Mountains, 14
Northern Basin and Range, 15
Central California Foothills and Coastal Mountains, 16
Central California Valley, 17
Central Basin and Range, 18
Sonoran Basin and Range, 19

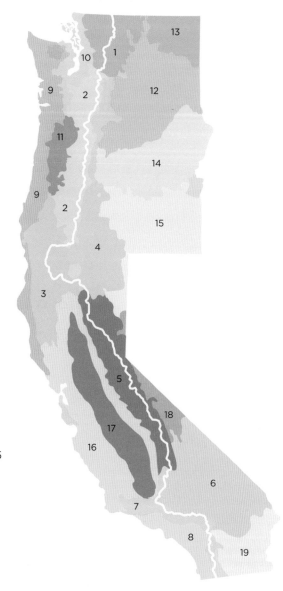

Elevation Profile

Laguna Mountains
San Jacintos
San Bernardinos
San Gabriels
Tehachapi Mountains
Sierra High Passes
Sonora Pass

SOUTHERN CALIFORNIA

CENTRAL CALIFORNIA

Some Sign Shapes of the Pacific Crest Trail

The current Forest Service signage system can be traced back to the early 1960s and a man named Virgil R. "Bus" Carrell. Carrell clearly appreciated good design and his study included the following enlightened observations:

"Signs identify things for us and add pleasure to a trip. A name of a river on a map can increase anticipation, but it cannot compare with the excitement that comes with seeing the sign that says 'MISSISSIPPI RIVER, mightiest of all American rivers.'

"An identified landmark can have a special significance to the viewer. For example, a sign that identifies boundaries of the 154 national forests is welcomed by the sportsman who knows that here he can hunt, fish, or just tramp around in the forest and glades.

"If the sign has an understandable purpose, is properly designed, made, and appealing to sight and emotion, it adds to the security, understanding, and pleasure of the tourist."

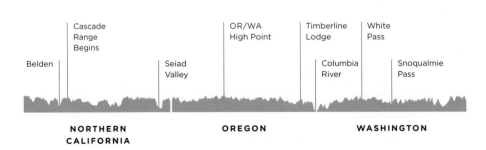

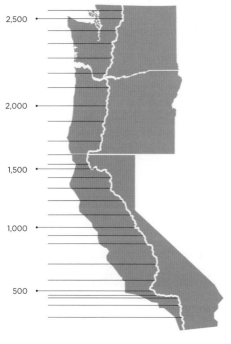

100 Mile Increments of the Pacific Crest Trail

Hiking the PCT one may come across mile markers every 100 miles, constructed by hikers and composed of rocks, pine cones, sticks, bark, and even lichen.

The Forest Service Logo

The Badge

A bronze badge featuring a fir-like tree symbolic of the nation's forests first appeared on the uniforms of Forest Service officers of the US Department of Agriculture in 1905.

The Shield

Known as the Multiple Use Shield, it pictures the badge enclosed by a ring on which is written wood, water, forage, wildlife, and recreation—the associated uses of the forest.

The Symbol

The National Forest symbol, based on a medieval symbol for wood, was created in December 1960. Five ovals stand for the five major resources of the national forests.

Of these three designs, only the bronze badge, popularly called "the pine tree badge" is still used today. When the Forest Service came to be in 1905, Gifford Pinchot immediately saw the need for both a unique badge and a uniform. A contest was announced and various tree-related designs resulted, including scrolls, leaves, and maple seeds. All were dismissed, as they lacked any recognized symbol of authority. The contest judges felt that the badge should evoke respect for Forest Service officers and their authority, particularly for those in the field tasked with enforcing federal laws and regulations.

One of the judges, Edward T. Allen, ended up developing the official badge himself. He felt that a conventional shield was necessary in the design. While at a railroad depot in Missoula, Montana, he was intrigued by the shield used by the Union Pacific Railroad. He traced the shield onto a piece of paper and added a large *U* and *S*. His associate, William C. Hodge Jr., sketched a fir tree on a sheet of "roll-your-own" cigarette paper. They overlapped the two sheets, quickly wrote "Forest Service" and "Department of Agriculture," and the official badge was born.

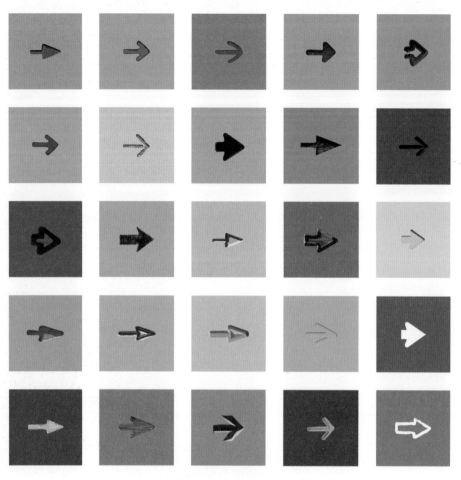

Trail Sign
ARROWS
FOUND ALONG THE
PACIFIC CREST TRAIL

An illustration, possibly by Rudolph Wendelin, depicting National Forest signage amidst a mountain landscape (Forest History Society, Durham, NC)

The PCT Blaze

The current PCT blaze and logo was adopted in November 1970 by the Pacific Crest Trail Advisory Council. The idea of changing the symbol or color in each of the three states was considered, but ultimately it was decided to create a uniform symbol for the entire trail. There are no details regarding the other designs considered, but it was decided that the alpine fir symbol being used at the time in Oregon and Washington, with an outline of mountains added in the background, would be the chosen design.

Rudolph Wendelin

Forest Service illustrator and draftsman Rudolph Wendelin was one of the best-known artists behind the Smokey Bear campaign. In addition to that work, he designed the Multiple Use Shield and Symbol described on page 11. In the early 1960s he worked as part of a group tasked with developing Forest Service symbols and signage that lead to the development of the iconic Forest Service script font and sign shapes. Images courtesy of the Forest History Society, Durham, North Carolina.

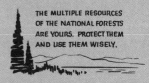

23

**NATIONAL
FORESTS**

Southern California

Angeles
San Bernardino
Cleveland

Central California

Tahoe
Eldorado
Humboldt-Toiyabe
Stanislaus
Inyo
Sierra
Sequoia

NATIONAL

WILDERNESS

Southern California

Domeland
Chimney Peak
Owens Peak
Kiavah
Pleasant View Ridge
Sheep Mountain
San Gorgonio
San Jacinto
Beauty Mountain
Hauser

Central California

Granite Chief
Desolation
Mokelumne
Carson-Iceberg
Hoover
Emigrant
Yosemite
Ansel Adams
John Muir
Sequoia-Kings Canyon
Golden Trout
South Sierra

Northern California

Marble Mountain
Russian
Castle Crags
Trinity Alps
Lassen Volcanic
Bucks Lake

Wilderness Signs

BY THE NUMBERS

44	42	2	6	5
WILDERNESS AREA SIGNS SEEN	MADE OF WOOD	MADE OF PLASTIC	APPEARED TO BE NEW	SEVERELY DAMAGED OR MISSING PARTS OF SIGN

Northern California

Klamath
Shasta-Trinity
Lassen
Plumas

Oregon

Mount Hood
Deschutes
Willamette
Umpqua
Fremont-Winema
Rogue River-Siskiyou

Washington

Okanogan-Wenatchee
Mount Baker-Snoqualmie
Gifford Pinchot

FOREST
AREAS

48
WILDERNESS AREAS

Oregon

Mark O. Hatfield
Mount Hood
Mount Jefferson
Mount Washington
Three Sisters
Diamond Peak
Mount Thielsen
Sky Lakes
Soda Mountain

Washington

Pasayten
Stephen Mather
Glacier Peak
Henry M. Jackson
Alpine Lakes
Norse Peak
Mount Rainier
William O. Douglas
Goat Rocks
Mount Adams
Indian Heaven

12	10	19	24	1
SEVERELY CRACKED	WITH NO HORIZONTAL DIVIDING LINE	ATTACHED TO TREES	MOUNTED TO POSTS	TIED TO A POST

Wilderness Signs

WILDERNESS

FOUND ALONG THE
ENTIRE PCT

WILDERNESS

BOLD/CONDENSED
CALIFORNIA ONLY

WILDERNESS

CURVED TYPE VARIANT
CALIFORNIA ONLY

WILDERNESS

PACIFIC NORTHWEST
VARIANT

WILDERNESS

MOST CURVILINEAR
PACIFIC NORTHWEST
ONLY

WILDERNESS

LEAST
INTERESTING

WILDERNESS

SHEEP MOUNTAIN
WILDERNESS VARIANT

WILDERNESS

HOOVER WILDERNESS
VARIANT

WILDERNESS

PASAYTEN WILDERNESS
VARIANT

NAMING CONVENTIONS

26	8	3	3	1	1
NAMED FOR MOUNTAINS	NAMED FOR PEOPLE	NAMED FOR LAKES	NAMED FOR RIVERS	NAMED FOR A FISH	NAMED FOR A MOUNTAIN AND A RIVER

SHAPE VARIATIONS

8 TOTAL	25 TOTAL	9 TOTAL	2 TOTAL

FOUND ALONG THE ENTIRE PCT   PACIFIC NORTHWEST ONLY

SAN JACINTO WILDERNESS
SAN BERNARDINO National Forest

SHEEP MOUNTAIN WILDERNESS
ANGELES National Forest

SOUTH SIERRA WILDERNESS
SEQUOIA National Forest

GOLDEN TROUT WILDERNESS
INYO National Forest

HOOVER WILDERNESS
TOIYABE National Forest

CARSON ICEBERG WILDERNESS
HUMBOLDT TOIYABE National Forest

GRANITE CHIEF WILDERNESS
TAHOE National Forest

BUCKS LAKE WILDERNESS
PLUMAS National Forest

CASTLE CRAGS WILDERNESS
SHASTA-TRINITY National Forests

MARBLE MOUNTAIN WILDERNESS
KLAMATH National Forest

SKY LAKES WILDERNESS
WINEMA National Forest

DIAMOND PEAK WILDERNESS
DESCHUTES National Forest

THREE SISTERS WILDERNESS
DESCHUTES National Forest

MOUNT JEFFERSON WILDERNESS
DESCHUTES National Forest

MT. HOOD WILDERNESS
MT. HOOD National Forest

INDIAN HEAVEN WILDERNESS
GIFFORD PINCHOT National Forest

GOAT ROCKS WILDERNESS
GIFFORD PINCHOT National Forest

ALPINE LAKES WILDERNESS
MT. BAKER - SNOQUALMIE National Forest

GLACIER PEAK WILDERNESS
WENATCHEE National Forest

PASAYTEN WILDERNESS
OKANOGAN National Forest

National Forest
WILDERNESS
SIGNS OF THE
PACIFIC CREST TRAIL

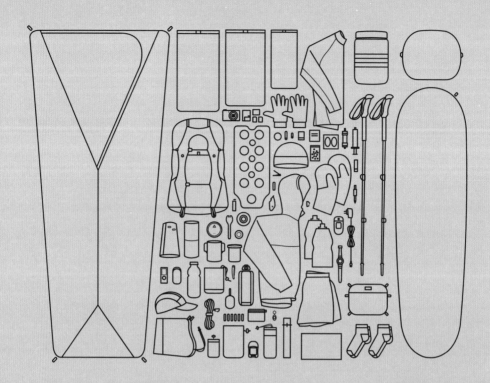

GEAR

Pack
Pack frame
Down quilt
Tarp shelter
Clip-in net
Stakes
Sleeping pad
Trekking poles

CLOTHING

Hiking shirt
Hiking pants
Underwear
Socks
Trail running shoes
Sun hat

CLOTHING CARRIED

Extra pair of socks
Sleep socks
Sleep pants
Sleep shirt
Rain gloves
Fleece gloves
Winter hat
Anorak windshell
Rain pants
Rain jacket
Down jacket
Sun gloves

COOKING & WATER

Water filter
Water bladders
Plastic water bottles
Spork
Screw-top container
Alcohol stove
Windscreen for stove
Cook pot and lid
Stove fuel
Lighter + matches

Notes
· Stove carried from Kennedy Meadows South to Canada
· Bear canister carried from Kennedy Meadows South to Sonora Pass
· Umbrella carried in Southern California and Washington
· Sun gloves carried in Southern California

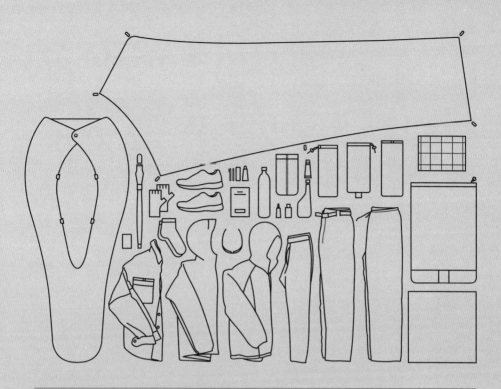

FIRST AID & HYGIENE

Deodorant
Razor
Sunscreen
Chapstick
Safety pins
Ibuprofen
Gauze
Moleskine
Leukotape
Toothbrush
Toothpaste
Hand sanitizer
Neosporin

ELECTRONICS

Cell phone + charger
Digital voice recorder
Digital camera
Camera tripod
Watch

MISCELLANEOUS

Chest pack
Inflatable pillow
Mosquito headnet
Backup light
Towel
Pocket knife
Bandanna
Wallet
Earplugs
Sunglasses
Stuff sacks

Dry bags
Maps
Headlamp
Umbrella
Bear bag hanging kit
Bear canister
Cannery Row
  paperback
New York Times
  Sunday Magazine

Gear Failures
· Pack strap broke in Washington
· Digital voice recorder broke and was replaced in Northern California

128
OTHER THRU-HIKERS MET

71% MALE

29% FEMALE

97% CAUCASIAN

1970   2018

YEARLY PCT FINISHERS

MAR   APR   MAY   JUN

HOW THE HERD IS FORMED
Thru-hiker start dates from the Mexico
border in 2015

TRAIL FAMILY

Thru-hikers often refer to their cohort of hikers as a trail family. Some may fall into a group in the desert and remain together for the entirety of the trail. Others may repeatedly fall in and out of different groups as they progress. Various factors may break apart a group, whether it be injury, a wedding back home, or someone quitting the trail altogether. At other times hikers may break apart only to be reunited a thousand miles down the trail. I witnessed one such reunion in Washington as two hikers who had not seen each other in nearly two thousand miles met once again. They tossed their trekking poles to the ground and ran toward each other to embrace.

105
AMERICANS

4
CANADIANS

2
BRITISH

8
GERMANS

2
DUTCH

1
SWISS

2
JAPANESE

2
ISRAELIS

2013   2018

**PCT PERMITS
ISSUED**

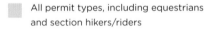

All permit types, including equestrians
and section hikers/riders

Northbound thru-hikers

Southbound thru-hikers

In 2014, 2,655
long-distance
hiking permits were
issued by the PCTA.
That number has
skyrocketed to 7,313
permits issued in
2018.

Hiking groups can also be quite diverse
at times, as people who otherwise have
little in common get to know each other
and spend extended periods together on
the trail. I met a group composed of four
members, all of whom were a decade
apart in age—ranging from their thirties
to their sixties.

BEST TRAIL NAME
Scotch on the Rocks
(thru-hiker wearing a kilt)

Thru-Hiker Archetypes

MOST MILES TO CONTINUOUSLY HIKE WITH THE SAME PERSON
Kennedy Meadows South to South Lake Tahoe

13

TOTAL (NON-CONSECUTIVE) DAYS WITHOUT SEEING ANOTHER THRU-HIKER

4

CONSECUTIVE DAYS WITHOUT SEEING ANOTHER THRU-HIKER
104.2 miles, Stevens Pass to Stehekin, WA

ALL THRU-HIKERS MET

Southern California
Angles
Apache
Baker
Bambi
Bird
Brainstorm
Brett
Carrot
Cheese
Database
Dewey
Doublecross
Ewok
Handstand
• Hockey (2)

THE ECCENTRIC

I came across a hiker who was carrying a steelpan—that large musical instrument with its origins in Trinidad and Tobago. It was contained in a thick fabric case and lashed to his pack with bungee cords. He carried a dead yucca plant as a walking stick, ripped up from the earth with its spiky leaves still attached. It was hard not to judge all this as affectation—a way for him to stand out on the trail. Some people, it seemed, had planned out elaborate new identities and unique ways of differentiating themselves from the hordes of hikers spilling north from Campo during those last days of April.

The following day I heard him playing his steelpan and the musical notes filled the morning air as I packed up. He was camped out of sight, lending to the eerie nature of the music. It wasn't the cheerful, rhythmic music one typically associates with that Caribbean instrument, but something more ethereal and much more fitting in the severe and otherworldly landscape of the desert. I dismissed my judgments and soaked up the beautiful atmosphere he had created.

THE WEED ENTHUSIAST

Further up the mountainside I passed a hiker. The smell of weed clung to him and he sat lazily beside a boulder. The sleeves of his plaid shirt were torn off to reveal a pirate flag tattoo on one shoulder. The brim of his hat was adorned with a plethora of bird feathers, each sticking upright around its entire circumference. He offered me a puff from his joint and I declined. "You're *craaaaazy*, man," was his response.

I CAME UPON a hiker as he sat blocking the trail, looking forlorn and completely exhausted and perhaps a bit stoned. He seemed to be in the midst of some internal struggle, and I felt as if I were intruding on him. He glanced up at me and the expression on his face communicated exactly what he was thinking. *Fuck, I have to get up*. He mustered whatever energy he had left and lethargically moved aside. We made small talk and I said, "A southbounder told me that the mosquitoes should let up here pretty soon." He stared at me with a look of confusion and was temporarily silent. "You mean, like, in a few seconds?" he finally asked.

ONE HIKER RECENTLY had a friend join her for a week on the trail. Another hiker, preparing for a similar situation, asked for advice about hiking with someone who was not a well-conditioned thru-hiker.

"Just go slow and smoke a lot of weed," was her reply.

He paused briefly and then explained, "Umm, well, it's my teenage daughter who's joining me, so . . ."

WASHPOT, A HIKER I had come to know throughout my time in Oregon, appeared from the trees and kept me company as I packed up. We talked for a while and he then asked politely, "Do you mind if I hike with you?"

"Yeah, absolutely," I answered, happy to have a companion.

He was friendly and positive—perfect attributes for a hiking partner. As thru-hikers often do, I asked Washpot how he received his trail name. Way back in Tehachapi, the story went, he was at a laundromat using a front-loading washer—the kind with a large round window giving view to the contents inside. As his clothing churned about in the sudsy water something caught his eye—a small plastic bag. It was his bag of weed, accidentally left inside a pocket. It worked its way to the front of the machine where it ended up plastered to the inside of the door. And there it stayed for the remainder of the wash cycle, visible to anyone who might walk by.

THE AFFABLE SOUTHERNER

I first met Lucky Strike as he stood smoking a cigarette on the trail north of Agua Dulce. He told me he was also from Virginia and had hiked the Appalachian Trail in 2001. As a child he would see the thru-hikers come down from the mountains and into his town to resupply. There were much fewer of them at that time, he said.

I saw him again much further north at the Peter Grubb Hut, a trailside shelter where we both stayed the night. As always Lucky Strike amused me with his jovial nature and quirky sense of humor. Another hiker teased him, claiming he survived only off cigarettes and Mountain Dew.

"We gonna have us a slumber party up there!" Lucky Strike called out in his Southern accent, nodding up at the loft. "You ain't gonna need your pee bottle tonight, Southpaw!"

He then elaborated on his custom of urinating into an empty bottle each night, saving himself a trip outside of his tent. "That's why I always roll out of town with *two* Gatorade bottles!" he explained and then lamented the fact that he had not visited a town since Tehachapi, some six hundred miles ago. He summed it up in a simple statement: "The shit-to-shower ratio is *waaaay* off."

Josh
Lauren
• Lorax, T-Fox (3)
Lost and Found
Lucky Strike
Leapfrog
Mary Poppins
Masshole
Mountain Spice
Not a Chance
Owl
Penguin
Periwinkle
Professor
• Rex (1)
Rudolph
Russell
Scotch on the Rocks
Sheriff Woody
Smuggles
Steady
Swan
Terry
Tim
Topo
Trek
Twice
Twinkle Toes
Uke

Central California
Almost Awesome
• Cracker Keeper
Crusher (7)
Darren
Early B (4)
Easy A
Ferntoe
• Freedom
Friendrick (6)
Gotta Walk
Halfmile
Hobbit
Indy
Joker
Micah
• Mike
Moxa (8)
Mr. Cup
Opossum
• Rice Krispie
Ridgerunner (9)
• Rocket Llama
• Rocksteady (5)
Salty (11)
Stumbles
Susie
• Thor the Hiking Viking
Whitewater (10)

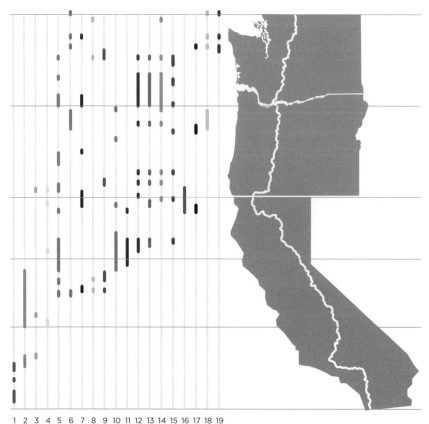

1 2 3 4 5 6 7 8 9 10 11 12 13 14 15 16 17 18 19

Who I Hiked With and Where

The thru-hikers I walked with for extended periods of time.

Some Conclusions
· For the most part I never encountered the hikers I met in Southern California again.
· Trail towns have a unique way of either reuniting or dispersing groups of hikers.

NOT-SO-SUBTLE TRAIL NAME FOR THE GUY WHO "HOTBOXED" THE MUIR HUT
In the Weeds

ALPHABET SOUP
All in the same morning I encountered three thru-hikers named Easy A, Early B, and DC.

INVASION OF PRIVACY
Seeing another thru-hiker's real name on his resupply package and feeling almost as if you've seen him naked.

MOST FASTIDIOUS INTRO FROM ANOTHER HIKER "Hi, my name is Goal Tech. Goal as in *goal-oriented*. Tech as in *technology*."

WHITEWATER WAS THE elder patriarch of the small group I had fallen in with. With this status, there seemed to come an unspoken rule that each night he would claim the nicest tent spot, private and removed from everyone else. When staying at a trail angel's cabin in Belden, just as on the trail, he had claimed the only private room, secluded and buffered from the din of the younger hikers.

Our group eventually dissipated north of Belden, but when I arrived in the small town of Etna I heard from other hikers that Whitewater had been bitten by a rattlesnake. Thankfully he was okay and had been recovering at the motel where I was staying. When I checked in I asked the owner, "Is there a hiker from Georgia staying here?"

"Oh, you mean Snakebite? Yeah, he's in room number one," she replied.

I knocked on his door and he brought me up to speed. Despite the misfortune of getting bit by a rattlesnake, he had actually been incredibly lucky. The snake had delivered only a warning bite—little, if any, venom had been injected. The rattler was also courteous enough to strike near a paved road where there was a cell phone signal. In addition to that, Whitewater had been around other hikers, one of whom was trained in first aid. An ambulance had come almost immediately. He would soon enough be back on the trail, his leg perhaps a bit swollen but no worse for wear, with a story not many other thru-hikers could tell. Word traveled quickly and nearly everyone in Etna seemed to know him as the Snakebite Guy.

AT DECEPTION LAKES I met a hiker resting beside the trail.

"Sorry if it looks like an Alabama yard sale," he said in a Southern accent, referring to all his belongings lying out on the grass to dry in the sun.

I laughed and asked him if he was from Alabama.

"Nope, I'm from Georgia, so we get to make fun of Alabamans."

He had thru-hiked the Appalachian Trail and previously attempted the PCT, quitting on the very first day. He had started much too late in the season and nearly suffered from heatstroke. Having already taken public transportation from San Diego to Campo, he found the same driver behind the wheel when he got back on the bus the next day. "I thought you said you were going to Canada!" the driver exclaimed.

Northern California
- Blue Skies (13)
  Colin
- Daniel, Red (16)
  DC
  Dirtwolf
  Farwalker
  Fat Dog
- Freckles, Jawbone (17)
  Gearslut
  Ghost Angel
- Grams (12)
- Half and Half (18)
  Handy Andy
- Highrobics (15)
  Johnny Rocket
  Lemonade
  Liverpool
  Marathon
  Patches
  Pig Pen
  Potluck
  Smokes
  Tarzan
- Washpot (14)

Oregon
  Bambi
  Barrel
  Ninja Tank
  Pip
  Sandman
  Shredder
  Sixpack
  Tartar
  Timberline
  Toto

Washington
  Atlas
  Big Sauce
- Bird Food (19)
  Buddy Backpacker
  Caveman
  Charlie Daypacker
  Irish Canuck
  Juicy
  Kimchee
  Lionheart
  Nobody's Friend
  Robin
  Safety
  Snail Trainer
  Strawberry
  Stringbean
  U-turn
  Watermelon
  Why Not

GRAFFITI

FOUND ALONG THE
PACIFIC CREST TRAIL

THE HITCHHIKER

At Little Jimmy Spring I filled up on water and encountered a disgruntled hiker who was not in the least bit enjoying himself. He had a permanent scowl etched on his face and seemed at odds with the world. I would come to encounter him often throughout Southern California. Each time we met I would hike on and leave him behind, but despite that a day or two later I would inevitably arrive in a town only to find him already there.

At the Mill Creek Summit Fire Station a hiker arrived with his headlamp on, like a cyclops emerging from the inky darkness. He either forgot about, or had no interest in, turning off the light and proceeded to blind anyone who looked his way in the hopes of discerning his identity. People greeted the newcomer and received only silence in return. It turned out, unsurprisingly, to be the hiker I met at the spring, and he was in a fouler mood than before because of the relentless descent down Pacifico Mountain. He disappeared into the shadows, hunched over and despondent at the edge of a picnic table. Later when a hiker asked with concern where he was, he gave no response. She finally noticed him in the shadows and asked about his day.

"Don't you worry about me," he responded with contempt.

The following morning I overheard him arguing passionately with another hiker about whether the moon was waxing or waning.

In Kennedy Meadows I came upon land owned by a local trail angel—a piece of property with a cluster of trailers, RVs, and campers. It seemed to be deserted. I wandered around the property but soon realized I was not alone. A figure lurked inside one of the dark structures. There was something familiar about him.

I realized that it was the same man I had left behind hundreds of miles ago, and yet once again there he was, having reached a destination long before me. I tried to strike up a conversation. "Is this place open?"

"Yes."

"Oh. I had heard it was closed down this year," I said, looking around at the empty property.

"Nope," was his only response.

I encountered him for a final time the next day as I hiked out of Kennedy Meadows. He stood alone in the middle of the road. He was surprisingly talkative and chipper as he escorted my hiking partner and me out of town so he could "see where the trail picked back up." We wished him well and headed toward the PCT. He stopped us, looked warily from side to side, then leaned in to confide to us in a hushed tone, "Dirty little secret . . . I may have skipped the last one hundred and fifty miles."

THE AGGRO HIKER

I found myself in a cool, shaded area full of sagebrush. The sunlight had yet to penetrate that little nook in the hills and the air retained the chill of the previous night and smelled of sweet sage. I took a sip of water and lingered a bit, then continued on. I saw a trio of male hikers ahead. One of them brimmed with energy.

"Oh yeah! Fuck!" he yelled. "Just gotta get out of this fucking canyon. Yeah! Gotta drink some fuckin' *agua* and get the fuck outta here!"

As I passed by he called out to me, "How are *you*, man?"

It somehow came across as more of a challenge than a greeting. I continued on, and as I climbed up a small rise I heard him pierce the air with a loud scream that reverberated through the hills.

THE CREEP

I first noticed him at a trail angel's home—he was a middle-aged hiker being scolded by a volunteer for not following the rules. He protested like an admonished child. Later, at Hikertown, he claimed repeatedly to whoever would listen that he had seen a ring-tailed lemur on the side of the trail—those stripe-tailed primates that live only on the island of Madagascar. He had watched them often, he explained, on visits to the zoo and there was no doubt in his mind about what he had seen. Someone tried to explain to him that it was a ring-tailed cat—a member of the raccoon family—but he would have none of it.

In Lone Pine I stopped by the youth hostel to see if I could stay for the night and inside I saw him, apparently in the midst of being kicked out. He protested as much as he had when scolded back at the trail angel's home. The woman at the front desk, however, had clearly made up her mind. She asked him to gather up his things and leave. The hostel had been fully booked by a large group and there was nowhere for him to stay, she explained.

Overhearing this, I left, not realizing the reality of the situation. The hostel had not been rented out; she was simply trying to avoid an altercation. As I later found out, this hiker, a man I assumed to be in his fifties, had made unwelcome advances toward a young female hiker. Once a seemingly harmless eccentric muttering about lemurs, he had now taken on a more malicious identity. I learned yet another unsettling detail about him further along the trail: he had supposedly cornered a hiker to rant about his disdain for miscegenation. In addition, he claimed to appreciate David Duke's ideas, though he conceded they were perhaps "a little extreme."

THE TRUST FUNDER

I stood at the California/Oregon border. I had spent eighty-seven days walking the length of an entire state. Washington lay 498 trail miles north of where I stood. Canada lay 464 miles beyond that. I stood there reading the trail register and noticed the epigraph page from *One Flew Over the Cuckoo's Nest*, which had been torn out and taped into the register, a fitting welcome to Oregon from famous Oregonian writer Ken Kesey. On the yellowed fragment of paper, typeset in an italicized serif font, were the lyrics "One flew east, one flew west, one flew over the cuckoo's nest." Scrawled in pen above it was a message from another thru-hiker: "Welcome to Oregon, hiker trash."

The message was signed by a thru-hiker whose name I recognized. I had only met him briefly, just before Etna. He seemed just like any other male thru-hiker, bearded and filthy. According to other hikers, however, he, along with everyone in his family, had never needed to work a day in their lives. He had a trust fund and his family administered a foundation that donated millions of dollars to various charities each year.

I took my first steps along the trail in Oregon thinking about this hiker and tried to imagine what it must be like to never have to worry about money—what a different experience the PCT must be for him. The trail curved around Silver Fork Basin and a variation on the nursery rhyme entered my mind: "One hiked north, one hiked south, one hiked with a silver spoon in his mouth."

THE OBNOXIOUSLY CHIPPER HIKER

An elfin woman in possession of seemingly boundless energy could hardly stand still as the rest of us caught our

Old BEER CANS

FOUND ALONG THE PACIFIC CREST TRAIL

EPHEMERA
of the
PACIFIC CREST TRAIL

Please!
CLOSE THE
GATE

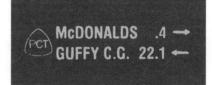

Angeles
National
Forest

MEXICAN
AMERICAN
FOOD

breath at the pass. She scampered about, jumping off rocks and yelling out, "Wheee! I'm doing parkour!" Later, as we ate dinner, she sat next to me shoveling instant mashed potatoes into her mouth with a large stick. "I always lose my spoon!" she explained cheerfully.

The following morning as I begrudgingly left camp at two a.m. to ascend Mount Whitney, she was no less chipper and energetic than the previous day. She hiked incredibly fast and had soon passed me by. Each time she lost her footing in the dark she let out a high-pitched "Oop!" She eventually took a break and I caught up to her.

"Wow, it's pretty damn cold," I complained.

"*Hmmm* . . . no, not really," she countered. "I just changed the batteries in my headlamp and I'm super excited! Yay, night hiking!"

THE GEAR OBSESSIVE

I met a young German thru-hiker who harbored an extreme fascination with hiking gear and its weight, garnering himself the trail name Grams. He was obsessed with carrying the least amount of weight possible and his ultimate goal on the trail, so I heard, was to pack so lightly he would be mistaken for a day-hiker. "Pretty soon he will be hiking down the trail with all his gear stuffed into two plastic grocery bags—one in each hand," one hiker joked. Much further down the trail, somewhere in Washington, an attractive southbound hiker had caught everyone's eye. Grams's response, however, reflected an entirely different perspective. "Did you see how big her pack was?" he had asked. "*Oh my god*, she didn't even cut off her ice ax loops!"

I tried to fall asleep as hikers on every side shouted back and forth in conversation. The chatter soon trailed off as everyone settled into their sleeping bags. Yet only a few moments later the silence was broken by Grams as he announced loudly to no one in particular in his slightly accented English, "Oh, I just put my feet into my bivy and it feels quite nice!" His comment was met only with silence and soon we all drifted off to sleep as the air hung heavy with an oppressive heat that lingered on late into the evening.

At the Bumping River we lingered for a while, perhaps subconsciously resisting the passage of time and the inevitable end of the trail. A group of trail runners passed us by, traveling on their way between White Pass and Chinook Pass to the north. Grams disappeared after them, making it his mission to keep up with and perhaps even pass the runners. In the end he was successful, and it only fueled his thru-hiker arrogance. "That last guy was *soooo* slow," he said at the top of the climb.

It was one of his two favorite refrains: "That person is so slow" and "Did you see how big their pack was?"

THE THRU-HIKER FROM PORTLAND

One thru-hiker was dressed in a carefully contrived outfit. He hiked in vintage-style Nike running shoes and thick wool socks pulled high toward his knees. A khaki Boy Scouts–style shirt was tucked into high-cut khaki shorts that barely reached mid-thigh. On one shoulder he had meticulously sewn an American flag patch and on the other a Canadian flag. Atop his head rested a Stetson hat with a feather stuck in it. He wore fashionable eyeglasses and a large yet well-coifed beard. Basically, he was a Wes Anderson movie in human form.

THE UNPREPARED HIKER

Ahead of me on the trail was another hiker, a middle-aged man hobbling along with one knee wrapped in a brace.

"Hello there!" I called out to him.

"Oh, you startled me!" he replied.

"Where did you start hiking?" I asked, wondering whether or not he was a thru-hiker.

"Oh, *umm*, well, I don't really know. About twenty miles back I suppose."

"I mean, where did you originally start your hike?"

"Oh, uh, *ummm*, oh geez. I'm really delirious. Ash-, uh, Ash-, *ummm* . . . Ashland! Oh, I'm really bad today."

I was concerned by how much he seemed to be struggling. He said he was thru-hiking, but as he put it, he was "doing a weird thru." He had started out in early spring but took a hiatus to get knee surgery. He then got back on the trail at the northern terminus and began hiking south through Washington on snow-covered trail. He slipped and fell, cracking a few ribs in the process, and had to be airlifted out on a helicopter.

And now it seemed he had switched directions once again, getting back on the trail at Ashland and hiking north. There was a part of me that applauded his resolve, sticking with it after two major catastrophes. At the same time, looking at his enormous pack and watching him limp along at a snail's pace, I felt perhaps it was time for him to throw in the towel. We were only a few miles from a road and Crater Lake National Park. I knew he would at least be able to get there safely.

THE GHOSTS OF THE PCT

Outside I could see the wind blowing the rain and mist sideways. We had all slept in, while avoiding thoughts of all those poor souls without a roof over their head, packing up their tents in the terrible weather. It seemed almost too easy, being able to put on my rain gear in the comfort of the hut. I stepped outside and followed the trail along the outskirts of a meadow and noticed a woman walking through the grass. She seemed almost like an apparition. We were several miles from any road and she had no backpack or rain gear on, but I was certain she had not stayed at the hut the previous night. The fog obscured my view and she disappeared into the white.

I CAME UP behind another hiker, hunched over and walking with a stiff gait.

"Hello there," I said. He stopped, turned around to face me, then stepped to the side, offering no response.

"How are you?" I asked him. Still, no reply. I passed him and soon stopped to eat lunch. He came lurching by and only a few yards further set up his tent at the side of a dirt logging road. It was only noon and there were no views to be had, simply a dirt road and tree cover. It seemed an odd place to set up camp so early in the day.

I encountered many such men and women throughout my hike. They seemed unfriendly, miserable, and worn down by the PCT—walking almost zombielike along the trail. There was a desperation to them, and they often refused to respond to a simple "hello" or to even make eye contact. To me they were the walking dead of the PCT.

THE ALOOF MALE HIKER

I asked one of the men at the table if they were hiking the PCT. He looked annoyed by my question and answered arrogantly, "Well, *right now* I'm eating ice cream, but yeah, typically I'm hiking the PCT."

SNOW-SURVEY
SHELTER

TRAVELERS

WELCOME TO
KENNEDY MEADOWS

ECHO CHALET

USA

TIMBER
FALLING
AHEAD

ENJOY
THEM
AT A
DISTANCE

RESTAURANT

DRINK
ROYAL CROWN
COLA

BEST BY TASTE - TEST

PACIFIC CREST TRAIL
CANADA 1233 mi ⇨
⇦ MEXICO 1417 mi

PCT
midpoint

The Great Seal Of
X X
State Of Jefferson

OREGON / CALIFORNIA

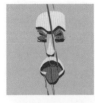

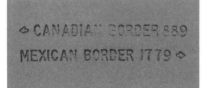

I ignored his pretentious attitude and asked if he was headed into the town of Mount Shasta.

"*Uhhh*, no," was the extent of his reply, treating my question as if it were completely absurd.

He fit a certain archetype of male PCT hikers—aloof, arrogant, and unfriendly, with a disinterested expression permanently etched upon their faces.

THE HIKERS MOVED over the area like a pack of feral dogs, clearing out brush and dead leaves, scraping the ground to mark their territory and create some semblance of a flat spot on which to lay out their sleeping pad. There were far too many hikers for such a small area, more people crammed into a campsite than I had experienced even in Southern California. I found myself among a large, tight-knit group that had been hiking together for quite some time. Some were friendly, but most were standoffish, somehow wary of new hikers they had never met before. Upon meeting one of them I said hello and introduced myself. He ignored my greeting, dispensing with the pleasantries to immediately ask me if I had seen anyone from his group of friends.

THE MISOGYNIST
Mansplaining Hiker: "You look like you've lost some weight."
Female Hiker (whom he has never met before): "Excuse me?"
Mansplaining Hiker: "Most male thru-hikers shed pounds, but female thru-hikers all seem to stay roughly at the same weight they started. In fact, most of them are typically bigger to begin with, but not you!"

IN AN EARLY edition of a PCT guidebook the authors include an implausible anecdote about a female hiker who, in return for food, supposedly slept with every ranger she met along the trail: "One attractive young lady carried only soybeans and powdered milk. She made it—but only after she'd stopped at each ranger station along the route for a few days and made it with the ranger in exchange for palatable food." Needless to say, this paragraph wasn't included in further editions of the book.

TWO MALE HIKERS spoke of how much they hated Cheryl Strayed's *Wild*, a bestselling memoir about the author's 1995 PCT hike.

"What is it you dislike about her so much?" I asked them.

"I don't know," one of them conceded.

"She didn't even hike the entire trail," the other hiker added, as if thru-hiking was the only acceptable way to experience the PCT.

You Have Become an Arrogant and Entitled Thru-Hiker

You see a family having a picnic where the PCT crosses a dirt road and assume they will share their food and drink with you. They do not.

***

Brewpub manager: "I hiked the Appalachian Trail when I was younger. If I didn't have a mortgage and a family, I would totally be out there like you, hiking the PCT."
You (thinking): "Is he going to give me a free beer or what?"

***

You feel an air of superiority over National Park tourists, day hikers, backpackers, and even section hikers.

***

While resting at the parking lot near Rainy Pass a truck pulls up and a woman asks if she can take a photo of you and your fellow thru-hikers. You stand there patiently as she fumbles with her smartphone for what seems like an eternity before finally taking the photo. She lingers and asks question after question about the PCT. You politely answer each one, all the while wondering what kind of food and drink she might have in her vehicle and why on earth she isn't offering you any of it.

Celebrity Sightings on the PCT

Halfmile
Creator of the map set used by many thru-hikers.

***

Scott Williamson
(Barely Missed Celebrity Sighting)
Rumor has it he passed through the Indian Heaven Wilderness when I was in the town of Trout Lake. Williamson has set numerous records on the PCT and has hiked the trail thirteen times.

***

Stringbean
Runner who set the supported speed record of the PCT in 2014.

***

Ron Strickland
Founder of the Pacific Northwest National Scenic Trail.

***

Buddy Backpacker
Six years old at the time; at age nine he became the youngest person to complete the "triple crown" of long-distance hiking: the Pacific Crest Trail, Appalachian Trail, and Continental Divide Trail.

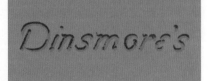

Trail Towns & Resupply Points

WASHINGTON
Manning Provincial Park •
Mazama •
Winthrop •
Stehekin •
Leavenworth •
Baring •
Stevens Pass •
Snoqualmie Pass •
Packwood •
White Pass •
Trout Lake •

OREGON
Cascade Locks •
Timberline Lodge •
Ollalie Lake Resort •
Sisters/Bend •
Various Resorts: Hyatt Lake,
  Elk Lake, Shelter Cove •
Crater Lake National Park •
Ashland •

CALIFORNIA
Seiad Valley •
Etna •
Mount Shasta •
Castella/Dunsmuir •
McArthur-Burney Falls State Park •
Old Station •
Drakesbad Guest Ranch •
Belden •
Sierra City •
Truckee •
South Lake Tahoe •
Bridgeport •
Kennedy Meadows North •
Tuolumne Meadows •
Reds Meadow •
Mammoth Lakes •
Muir Trail Ranch •
Vermilion Valley Resort •
Lone Pine/Independence/Bishop •
Kennedy Meadows South •
Lake Isabella •
Tehachapi •
Mojave •
Hikertown •
Green Valley •
Agua Dulce •
Wrightwood •
Cajon Pass •
Big Bear Lake •
Idyllwild •
Warner Springs •
Julian •
Mount Laguna •

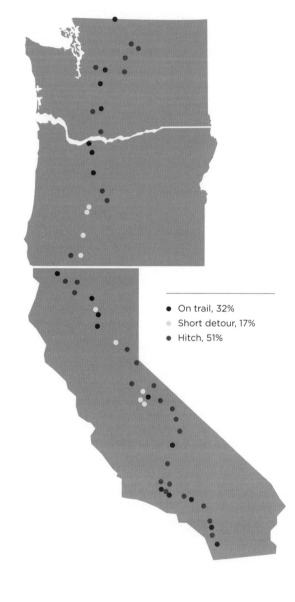

● On trail, 32%
● Short detour, 17%
● Hitch, 51%

Characteristics of a Great Trail Town
- Directly on the trail or requiring only a brief detour or hitch
- Compact and walkable, not too sprawling
- Decent options in terms of food and lodging, but not so many as to be overwhelming
- Scenic location
- Charming atmosphere
- Elements of Americana (neon signs, historic buildings, classic restaurants, friendly locals)

Best Trail Town
It's nearly impossible to choose a favorite, but considering the previous criteria: Cascade Locks, OR

Most Unique Location
Stehekin, WA

Hitchhiking

Hitchhiking can be a frustrating endeavor. Having grown accustomed to the complete and utter freedom of hiking along the trail, free from any constraints other than those imposed by oneself or nature, it is hard to suddenly be at the mercy of others. After so many days or weeks of unhindered progression you suddenly find yourself stationary at the side of the road, dependent upon the whims of passersby.

Most Intimidating Hitch
Santiam Pass

At Santiam Pass the PCT ends right at the side of busy Highway 20. It appears more like an interstate than a mountain highway as semitrucks hurtle by. At the most, thirty seconds passes between each vehicle, yet none of them are willing—or able, perhaps—to stop.

Best Music Heard in Someone's Vehicle While Hitching
Bob Dylan and Dire Straits

Kindest Person to Pick Me Up
A woman who put off her day hike to drive the opposite direction into South Lake Tahoe.

14
TIMES HITCHHIKING

44
MINUTES | LONGEST WAIT
Etna Summit

4
MINUTES | SHORTEST WAIT
Stevens Pass

STRUCTURES

FOUND ALONG THE PACIFIC CREST TRAIL

MOUNT LAGUNA
CA

WARNER SPRINGS
CA

IDYLLWILD
CA

SECTION D
CA

WARNER SPRINGS
CA

CAJON PASS
CA

WRIGHTWOOD
CA

WRIGHTWOOD
CA

LAKE HUGHES
CA

MOJAVE
CA

KENNEDY
MEADOWS
CA

MOUNT WHITNEY
CA

INDEPENDENCE
CA

LONE PINE
CA

To Idyllwild

The trail north from Highway 74 was closed due to a forest fire that had burned the previous year. There was no alternate route other than a narrow, twisting mountain road. Some hikers opted to take it by foot, unwilling to break their continuous walk from Mexico to Canada. It seemed to me a fairly unsafe option so I found myself at the side of the road with my thumb thrust out. A coyote slinked through the meadow behind me as dusk encroached upon us. It was my first hitchhike of the trail and so I felt wary. I was soon picked up by a musician headed to Idyllwild to play a gig he was already late for. An amp sat between us on the bench seat of his pickup truck. With the addition of myself and my pack, I was unsuccessful in completely shutting the passenger side door. I clutched the handle tightly, holding the door closed as we careened around one sharp turn after another, racing up the blacktop toward the tiny mountain town of Idyllwild.

To Mojave

A caravan of trucks passed us by, one driver reacting to our outstretched thumbs as if he had never seen anything so ridiculous. With an incredulous look on his face he flung his hands up in the air, the steering wheel of the massive truck left to its own devices for a brief moment, as if to convey, "How the hell could I possibly stop to give you a ride!" Another truck driver rose up and out of his seat, a puzzled look on his face as he leaned over his steering wheel to peer down at us like we were two hitchhiking aliens standing next to our crashed flying saucer.

Mojave Ted

In Mojave there's a local man willing to give hikers rides to and from town for a small fee. He will likely do most of the talking and perhaps having a captive audience is at least part of the reason he enjoys shuttling hikers back and forth. His father had worked at nearby Edwards Air Force Base, and he remembers as a child hearing stories about pilots crashing their aircraft. Supposedly his father would have to go around picking up body parts—a jawbone here, a leg there. One pilot, he claims, was so completely pulverized on impact that his bones disintegrated and with no skeletal system he was reduced to a blob of flesh on the desert ground. They tried to put him on a stretcher, but he slipped right through a hole in the canvas. When I heard these stories, I of course took them with a grain of salt, all the while intrigued by the fact that a father would tell such gruesome tales to a child.

To Etna

Traffic passed sporadically heading west, but no one seemed to be traveling the other way toward town. Standing there alongside another hiker, I had a clear view out over the road as it curved and twisted up toward the summit. It was silent and empty for some time, until finally we saw a distant truck making its way up the climb. We jerked to life and my companion pulled out a huge sign he had made for hitching. I had a small PCT bandanna with the words *Hiker to Town* printed on it. We readied ourselves, props in hand. The truck rounded a hairpin turn, then disappeared behind a ridge. Still out of sight, the sound of its engine grew louder and louder until it crested a rise and came back into view. Time seemed to drag as the truck approached and then slowed to a stop.

LONE PINE
CA

LONE PINE
CA

LONE PINE
CA

LONE PINE
CA

MUIR PASS
CA

TUOLUMNE
MEADOWS
CA

SECTION L
CA

SIERRA CITY
CA

SIERRA CITY
CA

SIERRA CITY
CA

BELDEN
CA

DRAKESBAD
GUEST RANCH
CA

OLD STATION
CA

CASTELLA
CA

MOUNT SHASTA
CA

ETNA
CA

ETNA
CA

ETNA
CA

The driver just sat there staring at us from behind the wheel. I stepped up to the window and he rolled it down.

"Umm, are you headed to Etna?" I asked.

"Yup."

"Okay, thanks for stopping for us."

We threw our packs in the bed of the pickup truck and filed into the cab, all three of us lined up in a row along the bench seat. Two small puppies squirmed and twisted and clawed and toppled all over us. They licked the sweat from my hands and clothing, crawled up my chest and shoulder, nearly fell out of the open window, tumbled back upon each other, and then repeated the entire routine again and again.

To Stevens Pass

I woke early, eager to hitch out and get ahead of the large group of hikers that had trickled into the Dinsmores. Just as day broke, while everyone else still slept, I stood at the highway and put out my thumb. A pair of moose antlers hung above the entrance of the nearby store and two swallows sat perched atop the apex of each antler, working in unison to uphold the already existing symmetry. Only a few minutes passed before a massive pickup truck came to a halt. I thanked the man for stopping.

"That's alright. I been in your situation plenty of times," he told me.

He was a Vietnam veteran and worked on a ranch in North Dakota. A cowboy hat lay upon his dashboard and between us rested a large hunting knife, sheathed and positioned in the center console. I felt uneasy at first but figured that with it there directly between us, he was trusting me as much as I was trusting him. Behind us in the truck's extended cab lay a dog and as we pulled out onto the highway she rose up and rested her graying snout upon my shoulder. I reached back to pet her.

"Nope! Don't do that!" he shouted at me. "She's a service dog."

He scolded her and she retreated to her nest of blankets.

"You traveling?" he asked me. "Or do you work up at the pass?"

"No," I answered, "I'm hiking a long-distance trail that runs from Mexico to Canada."

"Well, you might be just about crazy as me. Might even be crazier! When I was fifteen I rode a horse along the Nez Perce Trail from Oregon to Montana."

A large semi passed us, and the man picked up his CB radio.

"You on there, big truck?" he called out.

As we both waited in silence for the trucker to respond, my water bottles let out a loud pop, pressurized and expanding from the change in elevation. The man jumped in his seat, startled by the sudden noise. We slowly made our way up to the crest of Highway 2. When we arrived at the pass he asked me, "You got any munchies? I've got some Granny Smiths from my sister's yard." I thanked him for the apple and the ride, and we wished each other safe travels. I watched as he merged back onto the highway, moving on east toward North Dakota. I stood for a while admiring a wood carving by a local Tulalip artist, then turned north, crossed the highway, and rejoined the trail.

ASHLAND
OR

TIMBERLINE LODGE
OR

SISTERS
OR

CASCADE LOCKS
OR

TROUT LAKE
WA

GOVERNMENT
MEADOW
WA

BARING
WA

STEHEKIN
WA

Overheard on the Trail

As I entered a mountaintop landscape full of blackened and burnt forest—remnants of a wildfire—the wind picked up to speeds I had never experienced. I leaned sharply into the gale as I pressed on. My mood dropped severely and so too did my confidence. I convinced myself I would never find anywhere sheltered to camp. I questioned if I was even capable of hiking the PCT. I neared a road and a car passed by. A voice bellowed from the open window and before registering what had been said, my immediate reaction was to assume I was being ridiculed. Why else do people in cars yell out at pedestrians but to heckle them? A second or two passed before I realized what had actually been shouted. Carried on the wind was a single encouraging exclamation: "Going to Canada! Yeah! Do it!" That simple comment from a stranger had more of an effect on my morale than he could have ever known.

"You know you picked the harder route going on the John Muir Trail alternate? If I was hiking three thousand miles I'd sure as shit take the easier way!"

In the Mount Shasta Library a group of vagrant men in their early twenties sat at the computer terminals, typing away with hands stained black from dirt and campfire smoke. One of them had a giant backpack and the librarian asked him to leave it outside.

"What if it gets stolen?" he protested. "It's, like, my house, man!"

"I hear you spent an hour in her bathroom trying to find your hole."
(Note: If you have a slow leak in your sleeping pad fill up a motel bathtub and submerge your inflated sleeping pad in the water. Locate the source of the leak by looking for tiny bubbles escaping from the sleeping pad. Try not to take an hour to find it.)

As thru-hikers often do, I had hiked until it grew dark and simply set up camp wherever I happened to find myself, in this case not far from Highway 140. In the morning, two local hikers passed by as I was packing up.

"Wow, this is a nice spot," one of them said sarcastically. "You can *almost* not hear the highway . . ."

I hiked the last few miles to Stevens Pass past tents full of sleeping hikers, my pack lighter than it had ever been—a few bars being all that was left in my food bag. I saw two backpackers, loaded down with a week's worth of food. "I hate those thru-hikers and their tiny packs," one of them muttered under his breath.

A hiker had plans to meet his family at a trail town but failed to show up by his ETA. The family had plastered posters everywhere advertising him as a missing hiker. When he finally arrived a few days later he stared at the posters looking like wanted signs from the Old West and mused to himself, "I guess I was wanted for hiking too slow."

The Unexpected

SOUTHERN CALIFORNIA

Neatly placed alongside the trail were a pair of cowboy boots, socks, water bottles, binoculars, and two empty tin cans—one Vienna sausages and the other sardines. I could only assume they had belonged to a traveler who had slipped across the border from Mexico.

As I pressed further into the hills, I could hear the roaring sound of engines. The trail met with a dirt road that climbed steeply toward the crest of a hill. Jeeps, pickup trucks, and other more obscure off-road vehicles waited for their turn to plow up the incline until they lost momentum and power, their tires left spinning as they clung precariously to the hillside at a near-vertical angle. Only a few more degrees it seemed and they would flip over backward, toppling down toward the crowd gathered below. I stood with two other hikers looking on, somewhat bewildered. *What an odd way to spend your time,* I thought, knowing full well they could say the same of us.

A fifteen-hundred-year-old limber pine tree on Mount Baden-Powell.

Hanging unceremoniously from a tree branch was a cow skull that served as a makeshift trail register, covered in the names of hikers I knew and of those I would meet a thousand miles down the trail.

A side trail turns off the PCT and leads down to Joshua Tree Spring. The spring water is piped into a long stonework trough and is rumored to contain uranium—trace amounts that will only harm you if you drink from the spring every day, reputable sources contend. Water striders float on its surface and birds such as western tanagers and Steller's jays show no fear of the water, nor any hesitation in sharing the desert oasis with thirsty hikers.

CENTRAL CALIFORNIA

Still getting blisters after nine hundred miles.

An unattended rake on the trail.

WRIGHTWOOD
CA

LONE PINE
CA

A smashed guitar hanging from a tree.

License plate fragments, some dated as old as 1941, piercing the trunks of trees lining the trail. They are placed high up on the trunks, most likely serving as blazes for winter travel when heavy snowpack obscures the trail. They look, however, like shrapnel dispersed through the forest by a giant explosion.

A note on the trail in the Sierras left by a hiker the previous summer. How did it remain there despite the wind and a full winter of inclement weather and heavy snow?

While hitching from Sonora Pass to Kennedy Meadows North, I saw a dead chipmunk on the side of the road. Another chipmunk stood above it, looking down at its deceased companion.

NORTHERN CALIFORNIA

A huge, sprawling pile of trash next to the trail north of Belden, far from any road access. It included a tarp, tent, various books, scattered litter, and bags tied to trees.

The front half of a pickup truck sitting in the trees below the trail.

A ladder straddling the trail, as if to test how superstitious each passing hiker might be.

The famous railway bridge from the film *Stand by Me*.

In the middle of the forest, right next to the trail: a pantry full of food, a picnic table, an outdoor shower, and two trail angels playing the spoons and harmonica along with the radio.

Two people camped with their alpacas, playing didgeridoos.

OREGON

A potato sitting in the middle of the trail.

As I skirted the edge of private property I was watched by wooden posts carved in an appropriated Polynesian style. Frightening humanoid faces with tongues stuck out like some pantomime of Maori warriors glared at me as I passed. Carved messages warned:

LONE PINE
CA

Keep out, I see you and *If you can read this, you are in range*. A biker pulled up along the adjacent road and got off his motorcycle.

"What the hell is this place?" he asked me rhetorically and we both stood there perplexed.

Graffiti on a large boulder left by Boy Scout Troop 171 from Eugene, Oregon, dated August 2, 1960 (I hope they earned their graffiti merit badges).

A pile of fur next to the jawbone of a mountain goat, bleached white from the sun. According to a Forest Service ranger a pair of mountain goats had been rein-troduced to the area and the jawbone belonged to the female—she had been recently killed by a cougar. A little further down the trail I met two thru-hikers. One of them was named Jawbone.

A chipmunk passed through my camp-site somehow holding an entire graham cracker in its mouth. As it scurried past and my angle of view changed, all I could see was a graham cracker with a tail speeding along across the ground.

I passed into the Warm Springs Reservation and directly through a recently burned area. Smoke rose up from the still-smoldering forest floor and a fire crew stood huddled on a gravel road running perpendicular to the PCT. Fire hoses stretched down the length of the road in both directions, as far as I could see. There was a defined edge to where the fire had been halted, just a few yards east of the trail. The trees to the west had been untouched by the flames yet every needle had turned dry and brown and brittle.

WASHINGTON

Just past the road, in the shadow of Mount Adams, a hand-written sign directed us toward trail magic. In a

LONE PINE
CA

nearby car camping site, a man named Wagon Wheel, who had thru-hiked the trail the previous year, had set up shop. He offered us beer, doughnuts, and the pièce de résistance—grilled cheese. As I talked with him, I wondered why his name sounded so familiar and then I realized it—near the thousand-mile mark in the Sierras I had discovered a note from the previous year, left for a hiker named Wagon Wheel. They were, it turned out, one in the same.

Still getting blisters.

At Cady Pass in Section K, there stands a large tree. A century ago travelers from nearby Lake Wenatchee, most likely sheepherders, had stripped away its bark and carved their names into its trunk. The tree is slowly reclaiming this exposed scar and eventually the names will disappear altogether, enveloped by the tree. For now, their carving is still partially visible. They carved *Lake Wenatchee* and their names, which appear to be D. S. Rice and W. P. Hart. It is dated 192-, with the final numeral already obscured by the tree's bark.

I came to enjoy the big climbs of the trail, once so dreaded. I tackled each one with a feeling of invincibility, full of energy and positivity. The final two sections of the PCT were a high, both literally and figuratively.

**Abandoned Belongings
Found on the Trail**
- T-shirt
- Sweatshirt
- Flannel shirt
- Reflective highway worker vest
- Decomposing sock
- Neatly folded jacket on a rock
- Pair of pants on a tree trunk
- Pair of shorts
- T-shirt for the metal band
  Lamb of God
- Horse saddle resting on a tree branch

MT. WHITNEY MOTEL

Sno-Flake DRIVE IN
HAMBURGERS
HOT DOGS

LONE PINE
CA

SOUTH LAKE TAHOE
CA

PCT Pet Peeves

Hikers who refuse to say hello or even make eye contact.

Having to stop to dig a cathole only a few miles from a town, where there is the luxury of a flush toilet.

Spending ten minutes trying to fill your water bottle from a tiny trickle of water, then coming across a gushing spring just around the bend.

Feeling like you have carried too much food out of town.

Not being able to find a flat spot to camp as the sun begins to set.

Deciding not to set up your tarp and then worrying all night that it may rain.

Being visited during the night by an animal that chews holes in the sweat-stained wrist straps of your trekking poles in search of salt.

The constant repetition of things day after day on the trail can arouse feelings of annoyance. Wind turbines. Afternoon clouds and thunderstorms. The yellow flowers known as mule's ears. There's nothing inherently bad about mule's ears—in fact it's a beautiful flower. Yet seeing it for such an extended period makes it seem not as if you are progressing, but rather that you are stuck in one place, unable to reach new scenery. Your experience takes on a Groundhog Day effect.

Waking up in the morning to a swarm of mosquitoes covering the mesh of your tent, just waiting for you to expose yourself.

Horse shit on the trail—especially when fresh.

The way time seems to drag on in the late afternoon.

Any time you need to retrace your steps, rather than continually progress north.

Trying to fall asleep when it is windy, as you lay in tense apprehension waiting for the next gust of wind to rattle your tent.

SOUTH LAKE TAHOE
CA

BELDEN
CA

MOUNT SHASTA
CA

The Simple Joys of Thru-Hiking the PCT

Finding an outhouse with toilet paper.

Taking off a heavy pack and feeling as if you are walking on the moon, bouncing with every step.

While night hiking, coming upon the luminescent dome of a tent lit from within by a hiker's headlamp.

Another hiker arriving at the top of Mount Whitney and giving you a huge hug, though you have never met.

Entering tree cover and experiencing the soft tread of a forested trail after a long descent over rocky terrain.

The smell of freshly exposed wood from a fallen and cracked open tree trunk.

Using your bear canister as a seat.

Reaching Sonora Pass and realizing you no longer need to carry a heavy bear canister.

How light your pack is as your approach the next town or resupply point.

Reaching destinations that once seemed so distant and unattainable.

Initially forming a bad impression of someone and then hundreds of miles later hiking alongside that same person for days on end and developing a rapport and a growing list of inside jokes. On a 2,600-mile hike, you get second chances to know people that you don't get in ordinary life.

Experiencing the landscape changing slowly while on foot, one mile at a time.

Enjoying the simple acts of eating, bathing, and sleeping in a warm bed that you can only truly appreciate when you have deprived yourself of those simplest of life's pleasures.

An expansive and unhindered desert vista.

MOUNT SHASTA
CA

Songs

WHY SOME SONGS GET STUCK IN THE HEAD

In the midst of
a road walk

The Magnetic Fields
"When My Boy Walks
Down the Street"

See an informational
sign about the California
scrub jay

TLC
"No Scrubs"

BIG ROCK CANDY MOUNTAIN

The song "Big Rock Candy Mountain" looped over and over in my head as I hiked, to the point where it became maddening. There should be a word to describe the sheer annoyance of hiking uphill under the weight of a heavy pack while the same song plays endlessly in the echo chamber of your mind. Fanning the flames, a group of hikers at Walker Pass sat in a circle playing a rendition of the song and I fantasized about smashing their ukuleles over the rocks.

As obnoxious as it became, I found myself relating to those lyrics sung by a nomadic hobo living out in the elements, dreaming of a Shangri-La full of every amenity that his current situation was devoid of. The song paints a delightful and evocative picture of a faraway land where "handouts grow on bushes and you sleep out every night." A place where lemonade flows from mountain springs and "the rain don't fall, the wind don't blow."

They may as well be the fantasies of a thru-hiker. I suppose Canada, which I hoped to reach in the coming fall, was my Big Rock Candy Mountain. Or, if not Canada, at least the next iconic spot along the trail. Perhaps Kennedy Meadows, that promised land at the end of seven hundred miles of desert—gateway to the alpine paradise of the Sierra Nevada.

ASHLAND
OR

See Young America Lake on a trail map

David Bowie "Young Americans"

Meet a hiker named Ghost Angel

The Penguins "Earth Angel"

Reach the two-thousand-mile mark on the PCT

The Rolling Stones "2000 Man"

Walk through a spiderweb on the trail

No Doubt "Spiderwebs"

Song Heard in Two Different Businesses in Two Different Towns along the Trail
Genesis, "That's All"

Most Appropriate Song Lyrics to be Stuck in Your Head at the Beginning of a Thru-Hike
"I'm a thousand miles behind, with a million more to climb."

Most Appropriate Song Lyrics to be Stuck in Your Head When Feeling Lonely on the Trail
"Damn you always treat me like a stranger, mountain."

Most Appropriate Song for a Road Walk
The trail gave way to road as I made my way toward Highway 96 and Seiad Valley. Music played loudly from inside a secluded home surrounded by a yard of tall grass—Metallica covering Bob Seger's "Turn the Page." The singer's voice broke the silence, "Here I am on the road again . . . there I go, turn the page."

ASHLAND
OR

CASCADE LOCKS
OR

Town Food

67
TOTAL PIECES
OF FRUIT

34
BANANAS

14
ORANGES

7
AVOCADOS

26
CAN SODAS

7
FOUNTAIN
SODAS

12
GATORADES

7
MILKSHAKES

12
PINTS OF
ICE CREAM

16
FROZEN
DESSERTS

4
SLICES OF
PIE

7
PIECES OF
CAKE

23
BOTTLES
OF BEER

11
DRAFT
BEERS

Food

What I Fantasized about Most on the Trail An ice-cold Sprite from a soda fountain, fizzy with carbonation and chilled with ice.

Most Memorable Breakfasts
Alabama Hills Café and Bakery, Lone Pine, CA
Morning Glory Café, Ashland, OR

Most Amusing Trail Town Restaurant Name
Señor Mr. Restaurant, Mojave, CA

Friendliest Service
Der Baring Store and Café, Baring, WA

Best Overall Food Experience
Timberline Lodge all-you-can-eat buffet, Government Camp, OR

Best Food Option in the Backcountry
Vermilion Valley Resort, Sierra Nevada

Only Meal I Couldn't Finish
Burrito at Roberto's Café, Mammoth Lakes, CA

Worst Meal of the Trail
Sandwich shop in Ashland, OR

I ate dinner with a group of thru-hikers at an Ashland strip mall restaurant near my motel. Our sandwiches were dry and flavorless, and our french fries were nearly burnt. There was no ketchup to mask the taste—all they could offer was a bottle of marinara sauce, nearly too thick to squeeze out.

The waitress made her rounds and commented, "Wow! You guys did a great job! You really cleaned your plates!"

I looked around the table, my eyes moving from plate to plate. Upon them sat half-eaten sandwiches and small piles of french fries. I looked up at the waitress and could clearly see the forced smile fixed on her face.

"It was very good," I said, as we all got up to leave. It was perhaps the first and only time a group of thru-hikers had departed a table with uneaten food left on their plates.

All-You-Can-Eat Buffets Along the PCT
Various casinos, South Lake Tahoe, CA
Round Table Pizza, Mount Shasta, CA
Timberline Lodge, Government Camp, OR

Food I Consumed at Timberline Lodge's All-You-Can-Eat Buffet

First Trip:
Potato salad
Pasta salad
Couscous
Lentils
Macaroni and cheese
Cantaloupe
Watermelon
Pineapple
Raspberries
Blackberries
Gouda
Cheddar

Second Trip:
Belgian waffle with butter and syrup
More fresh fruit

Third Trip:
Macaroni and cheese
Cookies
Chocolate raspberry bar
Miniature coconut pie
Chocolate cheesecake
Espresso cups filled with custard
   and berries

27%
BREAKFAST
FOOD

20%
BURGERS &
SANDWICHES

16%
SALAD

12%
MEXICAN
CUISINE

Town Food

65
POP-TARTS

30
DOUGHNUTS

35
HONEY BUNS

44
OATMEAL
PACKETS

14
INSTANT
PASTA MEALS

11
INSTANT
RICE MEALS

26
TUNA
PACKETS

25
INSTANT
RAMEN
PACKAGES

Trail Food

8%
PIZZA

8%
SEAFOOD

5%
PASTA

4%
ASIAN
CUISINE

11
FREEZE-DRIED
BACKPACKER
MEALS

67
TORTILLAS

10
PITAS

27
BAGELS

13
HOT
CHOCOLATE
PACKETS

40
SANDWICH
CRACKERS

205
ASSORTED
BARS

OTHER

Trail mix
Chips
Crackers
Cereal/granola
Cheese
Peanut butter
Dried fruit
Wild berries

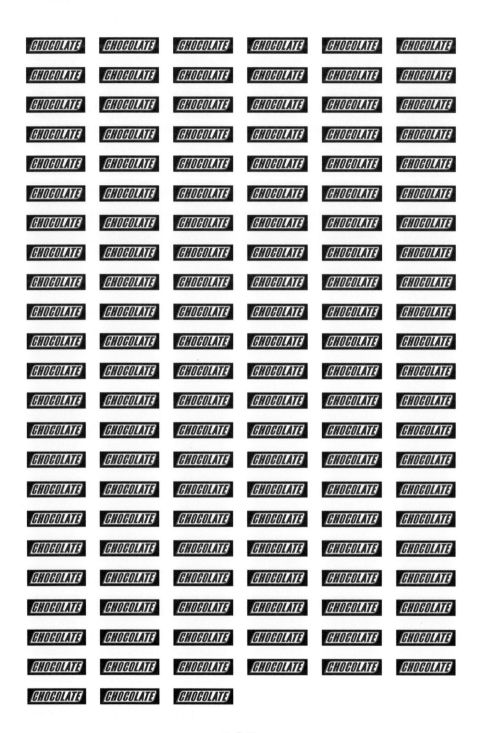

135

CHOCOLATE
BARS

More Simple Joys of Thru-Hiking the PCT

Reminiscing with other hikers about favorite trail towns and restaurants.

Experiencing the "blue hour"—after the warm tones of the sunset have passed and the sky returns to a blue color, though much more vivid of a hue in the fading light than the blue sky of day.

Camping on soft pine needles.

Changing into your sleeping clothes and sliding into your warm sleeping bag, as flashes of static electricity light up the darkness each time you brush against the mesh walls of your shelter.

Reaching the Sierras and no longer having to check the Southern California water report because water is finally plentiful.

Having endorphins dissolve your negative thoughts and worries.

The sound of a hummingbird's wings.

Finding a picnic table, railing, or flat boulder that you can eat at while standing up, rather than sitting in the dirt.

Arriving in town as early as possible in the morning so that you can maximize your time in civilization.

Finding a leaf that someone placed perfectly in the flow of a trickling spring, creating a funnel that makes it easier for you to fill your water bottle.

Passing the time by trying to picture every campsite you've slept at since Mexico.

Realizing the rain has finally stopped.

Hiking along the trail as you pass by tents full of slumbering hikers and feeling like you have the mountains all to yourself.

Hiking through a darkening forest at dusk and noticing the little spots of warm, rich light that make it through the trees and fall upon the trail.

Hiking through the berry bushes of Washington and turning around to find your hiking companions have disappeared because they stopped to feast on berries. Then you do the same.

Passing along a section of trail where crews have hacked away the thick brush that threatens to obliterate any semblance of a pathway. And even better, finding that someone has taken the effort to leave a solitary flower unscathed, while everything around it is chopped to its roots.

The sunrise.

The sunset.

Seeing a rainbow.

That feeling of wanting to be nowhere else than where you currently are.

Thinking, *Tonight I will camp in a different state.*

Realizing that wherever you happen to be, you walked there all the way from Mexico.

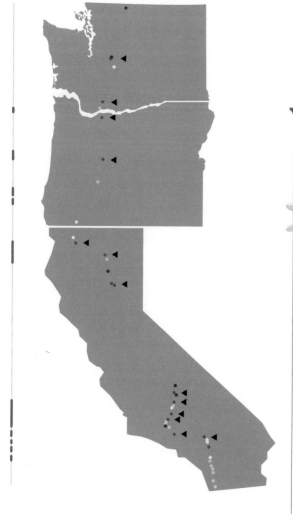

No Sadder Sight on a hot August Day An empty water cache and a cooler full of crushed soda cans, their contents long since consumed.

Water Caches & Trail Magic

- Water cache
- Food
- Soda
- Alcohol

◄ Trail angels present
– Dry stretches

Best Water Cache Kelso Valley Road, CA, where in addition to gallons of water there were coolers full of soda, juice, and even bottled Starbucks Frappuccinos.

Least Appealing Trail Magic Beer, spam, and Vienna sausages at Harts Pass, WA.

Living Vicariously through Others The visitor center was closed, and we met two hikers who informed us we had just missed out on trail magic. I asked about it, but they refused to tell me anything more. "I wouldn't want to break your heart," one of them said.

The Random Thoughts of a Thru-Hiker

Throughout my hike I felt oddly connected to my childhood. Is there a correlation between how we perceive the wilderness and the way we saw the world in our youth? Every day I witnessed something new and different as I traveled through the mountains with what could only be described as a child-like sense of wonder. Though at times I failed do so, I was more or less living in the moment—certainly more than I normally did as an adult. Like a child, I was concerned primarily with my immediate needs. Food. Water. Shelter. Finding a place to use the bathroom. For the most part there wasn't much existential fear or worry out there on the trail. Time passed slowly—the way summers seemed to last forever as a child—and my thoughts rarely strayed too far into the future.

I entered a lonely meadow beneath overcast skies. Ahead of me was a forested U-shaped valley. There was something dreamlike about the forest, as if it were not real but a painted backdrop. It brought about a vague memory of a television show I had seen when I was a child, which in retrospect seems fairly terrifying. In it, children were sucked into a landscape painting and forced to wander through mountains and forests without end. They were destined to roam an infinite and purgatorial landscape, never reaching any destination and with nothing changing to mark the passage of time or distance.

Should there be some apocalyptic event that wiped mankind from the earth, yet left the natural world intact, how long would it take for the forest to reclaim the PCT? When would it vanish completely, with no trace?

A seemingly incoherent phrase entered my mind and looped over and over again: *Tikki tikki tembo-no sa rembo* . . . It sounded familiar, yet I had no idea what it meant or where it came from. It turns out, as I later discovered, that it is from a 1968 children's book. It tells a fabricated and culturally insensitive folktale about the supposed practice of Chinese parents giving their firstborn son an elaborately complex name. I have absolutely no recollection of reading this book as a child, yet the phrase lay dormant in some far corner of my brain waiting for the silence and repetition of a thru-hike to usher it forth into my consciousness. I had forgotten the character's entire name, if I ever knew it at all: *Tikki tikki tembo-no sa rembo-chari bari ruchi-pip peri pembo.*

As I hiked in the heat along the dry, dusty trail I recorded my daily journal into my digital voice recorder. I gave a message to my future self: "Go to the fridge now, drink a cold beverage, and think of me."

Tired of the various challenges of the trail, I imagined myself a thru-hiking superhero with relevant powers:

· Always run out of food just as you reach your next resupply point, with no excess food having been carried.
· Always run out of water just as you get to the next water source, with no excess water having been carried.
· In the desert, always know which water caches will be stocked and which streams/springs will be running.
· Always know if you actually need to filter water from a particular source, thus saving time.
· Always know the safest and easiest place to cross a creek. Always time creek crossings for the early morning so that the water level is at its lowest before the snow begins to melt.
· Always know the most comfortable and most scenic campsite at which to end your day.
· Easily and quickly obtain a hitch in and out of town. Know whether or not the driver is safe.
· Know if there is a bear or cougar in the vicinity.
· Have perfect timing when it comes to long uphill stretches of the trail so that you are never climbing at the hottest part of the day.
· Always travel on snow when it is frozen in the morning so that you can avoid postholing.
· Possess the ability to let your body hike on and cover more miles while your spirit lingers to enjoy a beautiful view, eventually rushing forward down the trail to catch back up with your physical self.

PARADOXICAL FANTASIES

Normal Life	On the PCT
Fantasies about freedom, adventure, lack of responsibility, and time spent in nature.	Fantasies about a comfortable life, home, family, and career.

Paradoxes of the PCT

Starting your hike early in the season to avoid the summer heat in the desert, which risks getting you to the High Sierra before the snow has melted.

Trying to exist in the moment when at times you are yearning for what lies further down the trail.

Living out an idle, leisurely lifestyle while walking a marathon's length day after day.

Experiencing great freedom, though you are confined to a single, narrow path that demands acceptance of many unchangeable circumstances.

Enjoying the shade and comfort of tree cover, while cursing the lack of scenery.

Feeling so enamored by the scenery yet feeling so utterly exhausted.

Wanting to go slowly and savor the beauty while feeling compelled to hike as many miles as possible each day.

Feeling disoriented traveling in a car down the interstate at sixty miles per hour after traveling by foot for so long.

A	B	C	D	E	F
Agua Dulce	Blisters	California	Devils Postpile	Etna	Forester Pass
G	H	I	J	K	L
Goat Rocks	Hitchhike	Idyllwild	Jefferson Park	Kings Canyon	Leave No Trace
M	N	O	P	Q	R
Mosquito	Norse Peak	Oregon	Pasayten	Quiet	Rattlesnake
S	T	U	V	W	X
Stehekin	Tuolomne	Umpqua	Vermilion Valley	Washington	Xeric
Y	Z	A	B	C	D
Yucca	Zero Day	Anza-Borrego	Baring	Castle Pass	Dinsmores
E	F	G	H	I	J
Evolution Creek	Fuller Ridge	Glacier Peak	Hat Creek Rim	Indian Heaven	Julian
K	L	M	N	O	P
Kennedy Meadows	Lassen	Mojave	Northbound	Olallie Lake	Plumas
Q	R	S	T	U	V
Quail	Rainy Pass	Sierra Nevada	Thru-Hike	Ursus Americanus	Vasquez Rocks
W	X	Y	Z		
Water Cache	Xenization	Yosemite	Zigzag Canyon		

ABCs of the PCT

Created from type found along the trail
or in trail towns

YUCCA

BEAVERTAIL
CACTUS

CHOLLA

POPPY

COLORADO
FOUR O' CLOCK

DWARF LUPINE

PHLOX

GREAT
BLANKETFLOWER

PRICKLY
PHLOX

SPECKLED
CLARKIA

BIRD'S-EYES
GILIA

BUTTERFLY
MARIPOSA LILY

DESERT
DANDELION

EVENING
PRIMROSE

FREMONT'S
PHACELIA

DESERT
MARIPOSA LILY

WESTERN
WALLFLOWER

WHITEDAISY
TIDYTIPS

BIGELOW'S
TICKSEED

DWARF
MONKEY-FIDDLE

FLOWERS
FOUND ALONG THE
PACIFIC CREST TRAIL

SCARLET
GILIA

WAXY
CHECKERBLOOM

WAVYLEAF
PAINTBRUSH

DAISY

WYOMING
INDIAN PAINTBRUSH

LEICHTLIN'S
MARIPOSA LILY

CARDINAL
CATCHFLY

BROADLEAF
ARNICA

WILD
BUCKWHEAT

ROYAL
PENSTEMON

COLUMBIAN
MONKSHOOD

FALSE
BINDWEED

LEOPARD
LILY

COMMON
MADIA

CHICORY

FIREWEED

BROADLEAF
ARNICA

LARGE-LEAVED
ASTER

WALL LETTUCE

HAWKWEED

SEEP
MONKEYFLOWER

PACIFIC
BLEEDING HEART

ASPEN
FLEABANE

COMMON
VALERIAN

HAREBELL

PRINCE'S
PINE

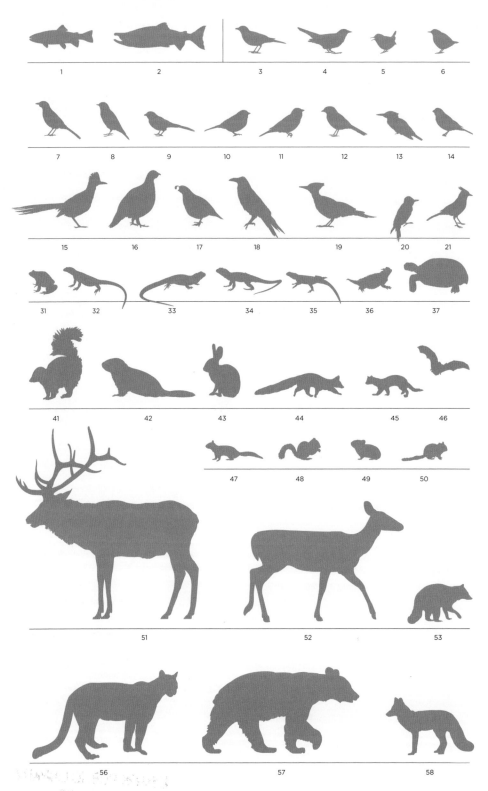

1   2   3   4   5   6

7   8   9   10   11   12   13   14

15   16   17   18   19   20   21

31   32   33   34   35   36   37

41   42   43   44   45   46

47   48   49   50

51   52   53

56   57   58

NOTABLE WILDLIFE OF THE PACIFIC CREST TRAIL

Fish
Golden trout, 1
Sockeye salmon, 2

Birds
American robin, 3
Red-winged
  blackbird, 4
Pacific wren, 5
American dipper, 6
California scrub jay, 7
Western bluebird, 8
Spotted towhee, 9
Dark-eyed junco, 10
Western tanager, 11
Gray jay, 12
Kingfisher, 13
House finch, 14
Roadrunner, 15
Grouse, 16
Quail, 17
Raven, 18
Pileated
  woodpecker, 19
Acorn woodpecker, 20
Steller's jay, 21
Swallow, 22
Kite, 23
Turkey vulture, 24
Flicker, 25
Eagle, 26
Hummingbird, 27
Great horned owl, 28
Hawk, 29
Osprey, 30

Reptiles and Amphibians
Frog, 31
Chuckwalla, 32
Desert iguana, 33
Collared lizard, 34
Western fence
  lizard, 35
Desert horned
  lizard, 36
Desert tortoise, 37
Rubber boa, 38
Gopher snake, 39
Rattlesnake, 40

Mammals
Striped skunk, 41
Marmot, 42
Desert cottontail, 43
Ringtailed cat, 44
Pine marten, 45
Brown bat, 46
Ground squirrel, 47
Douglas squirrel, 48
Pika, 49
Chipmunk, 50
Elk, 51
Mule deer, 52
Raccoon, 53
Mountain goat, 54
Bighorn sheep, 55
Cougar, 56
Black bear, 57
Red fox, 58
Coyote, 59
Bobcat, 60

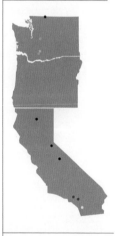

Memorable Wildlife Sightings

- Pileated woodpecker
- Elk
- Mountain goat
- Bear
- Rattlesnake
- Desert horned lizard

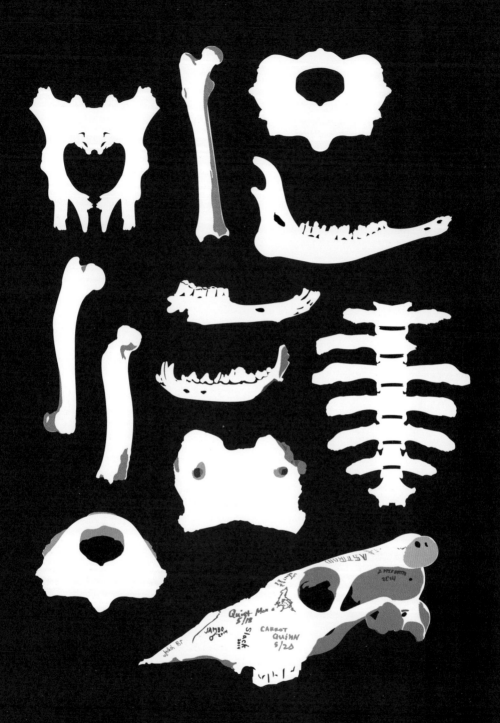

BONES
FOUND ALONG THE
PACIFIC CREST TRAIL

THE FIRST BEAR

I climbed higher toward Mather Pass, leaving the meadows behind, and eventually stopped to look back over the country I had passed through. I noticed something moving off in the distance, nearly the same color as the ubiquitous marmots, yet it seemed much larger. There can't be a bear at this elevation, I assumed, but I was wrong. It was the first bear I saw on the PCT. I watched intently as it lumbered along the rocky ground, dwarfed by huge boulders, and then I eventually hiked on, feeling the weight of my bear canister dig into my shoulders. It was most likely human food that had lured the bear so high above tree line, beyond the scope of any natural food source.

THE SECOND BEAR

North of Sonora Pass we postholed through snowfields and dropped below tree line into a canyon, soon calling it a short day as we set up camp in the late afternoon. As we talked I noticed movement out of the corner of my eye, down in a ravine below our campsite. Eventually I could no longer ignore it and walked to the edge of the embankment to peer down at the creek. Below us on the other side of the water stood a bear with his head low to the ground, looking not particularly ursine, but more like a large, shaggy dog. He had no idea we were there.

"Hey bear!" another hiker called out abruptly. The bear jerked upright onto his hind legs and looked around, sniffing at the air. It took him a few seconds to locate us and when he did, he immediately dropped to all fours and bolted up the opposite hillside. It was an incredibly steep ascent, but he seemed completely unhindered.

"I can't believe how fast he's moving," I said.

"Can you imagine if he had decided to run toward us?" another hiker wondered aloud.

THE DEER

We began an unyielding ascent and Rocksteady, one of the hikers in our group, pulled out in a huge lead ahead of us all. It was almost annoying how quickly and effortlessly he hiked. He had a spring in each step that made him look as if he were walking on air. His thin, ultralight trekking poles were like toothpicks, held loosely in one hand off to his side whenever he didn't need them.

Out of nowhere, I caught sight of a deer running at full bore down the mountainside above me. It made a tight turn as it met the PCT and shot straight ahead on the trail, directly toward the hiker in front of me. Just as I was about to call out a warning, it effortlessly dropped off the trail and traversed the sloping hillside below, passing around the hiker and then joining back up with the steep trail ahead of her—all without missing a beat. It was a breathtaking display of speed and agility and evidence that wildlife, as scarce as it is on the busy PCT, uses the trail in much the same way as hikers. Rocksteady had long disappeared from sight, and I wondered what scene would play out when the deer, with some difficulty perhaps, eventually caught up with him.

THE ANIMAL THAT RAN AWAY (THE THIRD BEAR)

Rounding a sharp corner, a dark shape appeared before me on the path—a bear lumbering southbound directly toward me. The animal and I seemed to notice each other at the same moment. Before I

Mourning Dove	American Robin	Red-Tailed Hawk	Clark's Nutcracker	Great Blue Heron
—	—	—	—	—
CALIFORNIA SECTION F	CALIFORNIA SECTION F	CALIFORNIA SECTION I	CALIFORNIA SECTION N	CALIFORNIA SECTION N

FEATHERS
FOUND ALONG THE
PACIFIC CREST TRAIL

35
FEATHERS FOUND

Steller's jay
MOST FREQUENTLY FOUND FEATHER

could lift a foot to slowly retreat the bear did an about-face and thundered back down the trail at full gait. He rounded the corner and disappeared, though I could still hear him for a while until the forest eventually quieted. The trail ahead curved at a 180-degree angle, and after a short moment I heard him yet again as he reappeared on the opposite side of a large gully, some fifty feet across from where I stood, careening down the trail. My nerves somewhat calmed at that point, and I couldn't help but laugh at his frantic departure and subsequent reappearance, sticking stubbornly to the manmade trail rather than fleeing into the brush and trees.

THE ANIMAL THAT STOOD ITS GROUND

I continued along the road to Castella when suddenly a bellowing dog ran out of its yard, stopped in the middle of the pavement, and refused to let me pass. I stood there at an impasse, trekking poles in hand as my only defense. The dog held its ground and bared its teeth, growling and barking. I had no idea what to do. Turning around certainly wasn't an option—even a snarling animal isn't

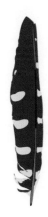

Great Horned Owl	Heron, Egret, or Bittern	Steller's Jay	California Scrub Jay	Nuttall's Woodpecker
–	–	–	–	–
CALIFORNIA SECTION N	CALIFORNIA SECTION N	CALIFORNIA SECTION O	CALIFORNIA SECTION O	CALIFORNIA SECTION O

enough to make a thru-hiker backtrack. Should I call the dog's bluff and proceed, hoping that it would retreat to its yard? A utility truck passed me from behind and the driver called out mockingly, "Use your sticks!" The man and his passenger erupted into laughter as they continued on. The dog briefly stepped aside to get out of the way then resumed its position.

I was relieved when I saw the truck eventually stop and begin to reverse, the driver apparently taking pity on me.

"Jump on the back," the man called out.

I leaped onto the small platform and grasped the hand hold. The dog watched curiously as we passed by, just as its owner came running out of his front door. I wondered where he had been for the past five minutes.

"He's actually a very friendly dog!" the man called out to us.

"Yeah, well he sure don't seem like it!" the driver shot back as we sped down the road.

THE ELK

In the Goat Rocks Wilderness, we stopped and stared out over a deep valley to the sloping ridge on the other side. We watched as a half dozen elk made their way in unison down the steep face of the ridge and descended into the forested valley below. With months of seeing mostly deer and marmot, it was exhilarating to see those massive animals traveling in a group down such dramatic terrain, one behind the other zigzagging across the slope on a faint game trail. Far to the left the white specks of mountain goats stood motionless on a ridgeline.

Later that night as I lay in my tent, I heard a rutting elk pierce the air with its bugling. It was an eerie noise, so oddly

Band-Tailed Pigeon	Pileated Woodpecker	Sooty Grouse	Great Horned Owl	Turkey Vulture
–	–	–	–	–
CALIFORNIA SECTION O	CALIFORNIA SECTION P	CALIFORNIA SECTION R	OREGON SECTION B	OREGON SECTION B

high-pitched for an animal that large, and like the creaking of some massive door being shut in the night.

MOSQUITOES

By the end of July the mosquitoes became slow and easy to kill. Often I would swat at one and watch as it failed to fly off. Unable to free its proboscis from my skin it became an easy target. At other times I would feel an itch on the back of my neck and go to scratch it only to find a mosquito crushed underneath my fingertips. The ends of my fingernails grew black with the remains of dead insects.

I could see their abdomens swell with blood and turn red as they sucked from my skin. When I smashed them the amount of blood that exploded was astonishing. One had made its way inside my head net and when I crushed it a thick drop of blood fell from the mesh. A mosquito landed on my right hand and I brought my left down upon it with a satisfying smack. I pulled my hand back only to reveal the mosquito still there, completely unscathed. Confused, I looked at the palm of my left hand and found a crushed mosquito. I had killed it, but another had taken its place almost instantaneously. I could feel them buzzing around the inside of my shirt. My legs itched with bites despite wearing pants—they were flying up inside my pantlegs to feed on me. On occasion I would pull a map from the cargo pocket of my hiking pants and find mosquitoes squished between their folds.

FLIES AND GNATS

Perhaps the one thing more annoying than a mosquito, and luckily much more infrequent, are the small gnats that buzz

Red-Shafted Flicker	Evening Grosbeak	Barred Owl	Grouse	Northern Saw-Whet Owl
—	—	—	—	—
OREGON SECTION D	OREGON SECTION F	WASHINGTON SECTION H	WASHINGTON SECTION K	WASHINGTON SECTION K

around your face as you hike, trying to enter your eyes, ears, nose, and mouth. They seem to enjoy pestering you at your lowest points on the trail, when you are hot, thirsty, and tired, and there isn't even the faintest of breezes to keep them at bay.

ANTS

Ants are probably the most ubiquitous insect along the trail. They are often seen walking in single file, following their own unique pheromone trails. There are the large, black carpenter ants that can be seen excavating fallen trees and carrying chunks of wood much larger than themselves. Leave your belongings unattended and moments later you may find them covered in ants. Brace yourself against a tree to dump rocks from your shoe and you may soon have a hand covered in ants. Set up camp in the wrong

spot and you will eventually receive an unwelcome surprise. Sit on the wrong log to eat your lunch and your meal may soon be interrupted by the sharp pain of an ant's bite.

I CRAWLED INTO my sleeping bag and noticed mosquitoes buzzing through the air. I felt a brief sense of regret for not setting up my bug net but closed my eyes nonetheless and attempted to fall asleep. I was distracted from time to time by the faint sensation that something was crawling over my skin, beneath my shirt. I tried to ignore it but soon a vivid image of ants crawling all over my body materialized in my mind. I struggled in the dark to find my headlamp and then directed it into my sleeping bag and panned the light across my body. I saw nothing. Then, after a few seconds, I felt the undeniable sensation of an insect crawling across my bicep. I touched my arm and could feel the ant's shape under the fabric of my sleeve, shocked by how large it was. I felt the sting of its bite and flinched in both pain and surprise. For some reason it let go of my flesh, only to latch on to my sleeve. I took off my shirt, turned it inside out and saw the ant there, refusing to let go. I flicked it once with my finger and its abdomen disappeared into the darkness beyond the light of my headlamp. I flicked it a second time and gone was its thorax. I flicked again but the head remained— the ant refused to let go even in death. I had to rip it off with my fingers. I took a deep breath and scanned the ground only to find it crawling with more ants. Resigned to my situation, there was nothing left to do but set up my bug net as I listened to my neighbor snore happily inside his tent.

YUCCA MOTH

Yucca blossoms off in the distance appear as small pricks of white against the dark, chaparral-covered hillsides—like the stars in a night sky. For millions of years, in the dark of the desert night, the snow-white yucca moths have been tracing out botanical constellations, pollinating the flowers and laying their larvae to feed upon the plant's seeds. They live in synchronicity. The moths emerge in spring from their cocoons just as the yucca have blossomed. One could not exist without the other.

VELVET ANT

Taking a break in the desert, the hiker may notice a large ant covered in dense hairs that glow a bright red. It moves across the sandy trail, burning with a vermilion hue as if its body had been set afire by the desert sun. The velvet ant,

also known as a cow killer, is actually a female wasp, devoid of wings and covered in hair. Though not particularly venomous, its sting is quite painful.

BAND-WINGED GRASSHOPPERS

When first spotted, band-winged grasshoppers will be fairly camouflaged, blending in with the color of the trail. When a hiker startles them, however, sending them into a frenzied flight, they spread their forewings and reveal their brilliant yellow hind wings in a clear warning to stay away. They land eventually, pull back their wings, and return to their former selves, their beautiful secret concealed once again. There can be dozens of them on the trail at one time, all forced into flight by a passing hiker. The alternate stretching and relaxing of their wing membranes produces loud snapping and crackling noises. They fly only ten or so feet further along the trail and land. This scenario can repeat multiple times as the hiker progresses down the trail before finally leaving the grasshoppers behind.

BUTTERFLIES

In Northern California a hiker may pass along the trail and suddenly encounter a swarm of baby-blue butterflies filling the air. As they sit still along a stream bank, they are all but invisible. With their wings closed they blend in with the ground—as the underside of their wings is the same color as the earth below. The vibrant blue tops of their wings are concealed as the butterflies sit in repose. It is only when the hiker startles them that they seem to materialize out of nothingness, bursting into the air like a tiny cyclone of fluttering blue shapes—fireworks erupting or confetti floating through the air.

Pale Swallowtail

Spring Azure

Northern Checkerspot

Variable Checkerspot

Western Sheep Moth

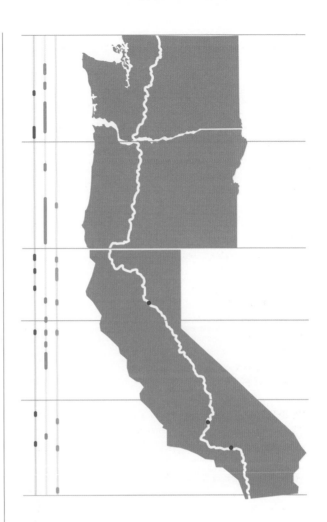

Insects on the Trail

 Black flies or gnats

 Mosquitoes

 Ants

• Bitten by an ant

Some Colors of the PCT

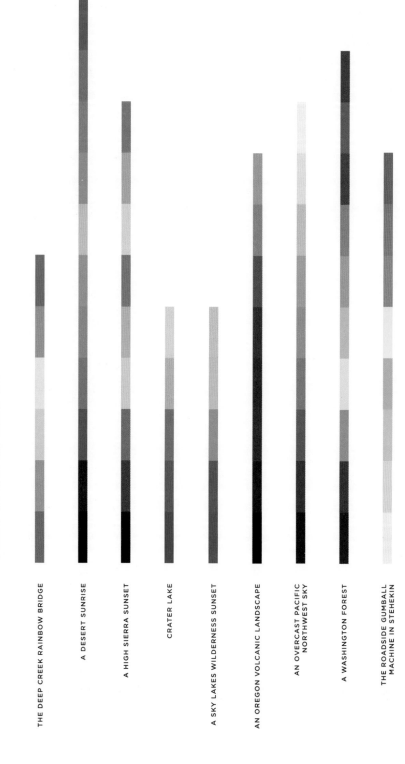

THE DEEP CREEK RAINBOW BRIDGE

A DESERT SUNRISE

A HIGH SIERRA SUNSET

CRATER LAKE

A SKY LAKES WILDERNESS SUNSET

AN OREGON VOLCANIC LANDSCAPE

AN OVERCAST PACIFIC NORTHWEST SKY

A WASHINGTON FOREST

THE ROADSIDE GUMBALL MACHINE IN STEHEKIN

Twilight

During a thru-hike, one has an opportunity to experience twilight more than at any other point in their life. Twilight (dawn and dusk) is the interval between day and night when the sun sits below the horizon, yet there is still light in the sky. In *Cannery Row* Steinbeck writes of this time as "the hour of the pearl," a time of great peace "when time stops and examines itself." In *The Grapes of Wrath*, Tom Joad calls it "the good time," when as a child he would get up and take walks by himself.

DAY		
CIVIL TWILIGHT	**Horizon**	
NAUTICAL TWILIGHT	**Civil Dawn** Sun is 6° below horizon	
ASTRONOMICAL TWILIGHT	**Nautical Dawn** Sun is 12° below horizon	
NIGHT	**Astronomical Dawn** Sun is 18° below horizon	

POETRY OF THE PCT

Hiking the PCT
Makes you tired and
sweaty
For trail magic,
Are you ready?

Signs announcing trail angels Ziggy and the Bear near San Gorgonio Pass

---

The Cascades are here
Lassen has many flavors
Try a cinder cone.

Haiku found in a trail register near Old Station, CA

Hexagon,
Octagon,
Oregon

Found in the CA/OR border trail register

I am one
who eats breakfast
gazing at morning glories.

Matsuo Bashō, seventeenth-century Japanese poet and long-distance hiker (on the wall at Morning Glory Café, Ashland, OR)

Stranger, beware,
leave not a fire,
foul not Mike's camp, raise
not his ire!

Mike Urich Cabin, WA

Obstacles of the PCT

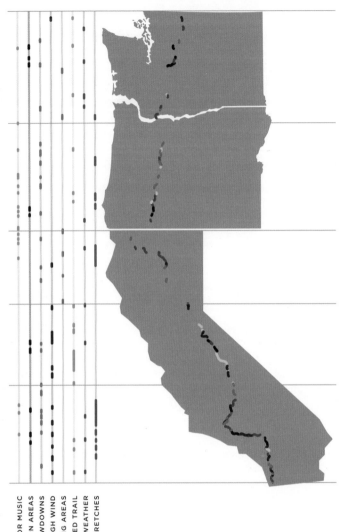

TIMES I DISTRACTED MYSELF WITH PODCASTS OR MUSIC
BURN AREAS
AREAS WITH NUMEROUS BLOWDOWNS
HIGH WIND
LOGGING AREAS
SNOW-COVERED TRAIL
INCLEMENT WEATHER
DRY STRETCHES

The Wind

In Southern California the wind turbines seemed novel at first, but soon lost their charm. They took on negative connotations as they came to symbolize that harsh and ever-present aspect of the Southern California PCT, without which they would stand motionless on the hills. They rotated and filled the air with what sound like eerie musical notes. I would often notice their movement in my peripheral vision, initially perceiving them as some large animal moving across the landscape.

The relentlessly frigid wind was a constant foe throughout much of Southern California and beyond. It tormented me throughout the day as I struggled across the landscape and again at night, keeping me awake as it battered the side of my tent. Caught on an open ridgeline or a never-ending exposed descent, I would wish in vain for trees or boulders—something, anything— to break the wind. In Northern California, when I finally got my wish and the winds subsided, its absence too was a curse as I plodded through the hot, stagnant air.

Areas Where Active Fires Were Burning
Hat Creek Rim, Northern CA
Mount Jefferson Wilderness, OR
Olallie Lake, OR

Most Beautiful Burn Area
North of Robin Bird Spring, Southern CA

All the charred bark had fallen off, exposing the beautifully weathered wood beneath. It appeared like a forest of driftwood.

Most Unusual Burn Area
South of Old Station, CA

The trees had been warped by the heat of the fire and they curved over the trail, forming an arched promenade of charred wood. Some were so distorted that their bent tops almost touched the earth, as if they were attempting to return to the ground.

Music

I hiked along while listening to music. As each song ended there would be a two- or three-second pause before the next began and familiar sounds filled my ears—my footsteps on the trail and the clicking of my trekking poles each time they struck the earth. In the absence of the music, the background noise of hiking suddenly became noticeable—crisp and clear and as if I were hearing it for the first time. Then the music would rush back in, filling my ears and mind and drowning out all else.

1.7% of my time on the trail was spent listening to music or podcasts while hiking.

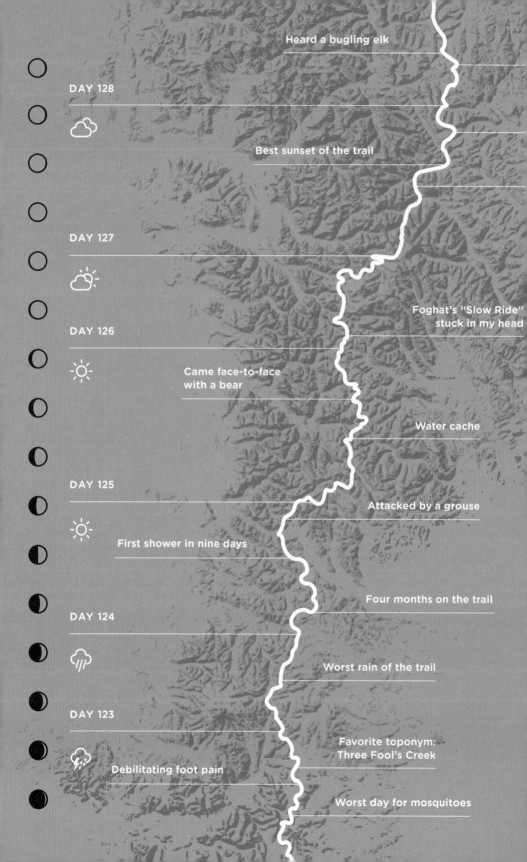

Heard a bugling elk

DAY 128

Best sunset of the trail

DAY 127

Foghat's "Slow Ride"
stuck in my head

DAY 126

Came face-to-face
with a bear

Water cache

DAY 125

Attacked by a grouse

First shower in nine days

Four months on the trail

DAY 124

Worst rain of the trail

DAY 123

Favorite toponym:
Three Fool's Creek

Debilitating foot pain

Worst day for mosquitoes

Saw a rainbow

Found a lost balloon
on the trail

Last blister of the trail

PART
TWO

THRU-
HIKING
The TRAIL

The Regions at a Glance	1 Southern California	2 Central California	3 Northern California
Begin	April 24	May 27	June 26
Finish	May 26	June 25	July 19
Number of days	33	30	25
Full days of hiking	27	27	20
Nero days	4	—	4
Zero days	2	3	1
Total miles	687.7	452.7	547.4
PCT miles	644.5	394.5	536.2
Non-PCT miles	18.3	56.9	3.3
Most miles hiked in a day	30.1	29.9	30.9
Miles per day average for full days of hiking	25.4	21.7	25.5
Miles of road walking	24.9	1.3	7.9
Elevation gain	131,951'	84,008'	95,337'
Elevation loss	128,753'	82,910'	96,451'
Most physically strenuous section	D	H	M
Sunny days	30	28	18
Rainy days	4	2	3
Cloudy days	3	2	3
Windy days	12	8	2
Snow | Sleet | Hail	2	1	—
Burn areas	8	3	3
Blowdown areas	4	4	2
Dry stretches	14	—	5
Off-trail water sources	4	—	8

	4	5
	Oregon	**Washington**
	July 20	August 9
	August 8	September 1
	20	24
	18	21
	—	2
	2	1
	445.5	520.7
	384.1	508.9
	55.8	9.3
	35.2	30.7
	26.9	25.6
	5.6	2.5
	62,001'	111,125'
	67,872'	107,422'
	F	K
	16	20
	4	6
	3	11
	—	1
	2	—
	7	3
	1	4
	3	2
	1	1

Stupidest Mistake
Drinking Stove Fuel

Lost in thought, I took a sip from my water bottle. The taste that hit my tongue was entirely unexpected. I spit it out and soon realized my error—I had just taken a swig from my stove fuel. Given that the fuel was perfectly clear and looked just like water, I perhaps might have considered putting it in a distinctive container or at least somewhere out of reach. I had not. I carried in the side pouches of my pack two identical plastic bottles—one filled with water, the other with fuel. I had given myself fifty-fifty odds and ended up failing miserably.

1 time accidentally littering
1 time finding unburied human waste
1 time driving a car
1 time riding in a boat
1 time riding a bicycle
2 times setting up shelter in rain
2 times hitting knee on rock when postholing
3 photographs photo-bombed by mosquitoes
5 creek fords
6 times falling asleep while hiking
7 movies watched
15 times watching television
17 nights before first camping alone
44 nights before camping alone again

Graphic Design in the Wild

Draplin Design Co.
Recovery.org logo on sign
California | Section H

Michael Schwab
Sugar Bowl Resort signage
California | Section K

	1 Southern California	2 Central California	3 Northern California
Times Dry Camping	7	—	3
Camped Alone	2	2	3
Times Night Hiking	1	1	—
Times Falling Down	1	1	1
Interstates	3	1	1
Highways	9	5	7
Paved Roads	25	6	18
Unpaved Roads	51	6	14
Photos per Day	13.1	22	11.2
Photos per Mile	0.5	0.9	0.3
Most Scenic Section	C	H	P
Least Scenic Section	E	M	O
Least Enjoyed Miles	413–444	1,001–1,018	1,423–1,476
Blisters	7	2	4
Showers	11	8	7
Laundry	5	4	4
Restaurant Meals	20	23	15

On Trail Shelter
Tarp + bug net
Bug net only
Cowboy camp

Accommodations
Campground
Trail Angel
Hostel
Motel

Waste
Flush toilet
Pit toilet
Cathole

Oregon	Washington	Physical Struggles
4	3	• Low energy, fatigue, and exhaustion
7	5	• Dizziness, blurry vision, and loss of balance
—	—	• Allergies
—	1	• Congestion at night
2	1	• Dirt and sand in nose
9	5	• Constant dripping nose
11	7	• Thick, dark, and bloody snot
13	49	• Cracked, bleeding nostrils
11.5	12.7	• Dry, bleeding nose
0.5	0.6	• Chapped lips
C, G	K	• Shoulder pain due to broken pack strap
B	H	• Itchy rash under armpits and on neck
1,840–1,859	None	• Chafing
2	2	• Ripped-back fingernail
5	5	• Cut thumb
		• Pain in right thumb
4	4	• Itchy feet and legs
13	11	• Knee pain

• Foot pain; blisters and rash on feet
• Ingrown toenail; cracked skin around toes
• Heels rubbed raw; painful calluses on heels
• Cracked calluses
• Blisters under calluses
• Raw, abraded skin on bottom of feet

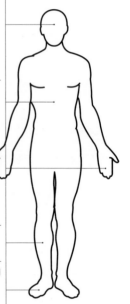

	1 **Southern California**	**2** **Central California**	**3** **Northern California**
National Parks		Yosemite Sequoia & Kings Canyon	Lassen Volcanic
National Monuments	Santa Rosa & San Jacinto Mtns. Sand to Snow San Gabriel Mtns.	Devils Postpile	Cascade-Siskiyou
State Parks	Anza-Borrego Desert Mount San Jacinto		Castle Crags McArthur-Burney Falls Memorial
Other Areas			
Daily Mileage			
Scenery photos per day			
Correlations Mileage — Photos —		1 2	
The Town vs. Trail Dichotomy	On trail	Gradually increasing dissatisfaction and yearning for the comforts of civilization	In town

4

Oregon

Crater Lake

Cascade-Siskiyou

Columbia River
Gorge National
Scenic Area

3

4

5

Washington

North Cascades
Mount Rainier

Lake Chelan National
Recreation Area

The High Sierra Slows You Down
Shortest Day in the High Sierra: 12 miles
Longest Day in the High Sierra: 23 miles
Daily Average in the High Sierra: 17.6 miles
Daily Average for the Entire Trail: 25 miles

**Most Physically Challenging Period
of the Entire Trail**
Day 38: Ascending Mount Whitney
Day 39: Forester Pass (highest point on the
PCT), Kearsarge Pass, and the long descent
down to the Onion Valley Trailhead

Most Uncomfortable Night on the PCT
Camping below Forester Pass on rocky terrain
in freezing temperatures

Best Sunrise of the PCT
From the top of Mount Whitney

Note 1
The High Sierra
creates an inverse
relationship between
miles hiked and
photos taken. The
rugged, difficult
terrain results in
fewer miles hiked per
day, but translates to
more epic scenery
and thus more pho-
tography.

Note 2
Two zero days in
Lone Pine.

Note 3
A drastic uptick in
the number of pho-
tos taken is explained
in four words: Crater
Lake National Park.

Note 4
An inverse relation-
ship is created in
Oregon. The gentler
terrain means more
miles can be covered,
but it also means
not getting above
the tree line and a
day lacking in views.
Therefore, on my
biggest mile day, I
ended up taking zero
photos of scenery.

Gradually increasing dissatisfaction and yearning for the beauty of nature	On trail	Gradually increasing dissatisfaction and yearning for the comforts of civilization	In town

Southern
CALIFORNIA
THE DESERT

[The desert is] a great and mysterious wasteland,
a sun-punished place. It is a mystery, something
concealed and waiting.

JOHN STEINBECK
Travels with Charley

FAVORITE TOPONYMS

Bacon Flats
Bucksnort Mountain
Burning Moscow
  Spring
Catclaw Flat
Champagne Spring
Cigarette Hills

Cloudburst Canyon
Coon Creek Jumpoff
Devils Slide Trail
Fiddleneck Spring
Hideaway Canyon
Horsethief Canyon
Jawbone Canyon

Lightning Gulch
Little Burnt Peak
Little Jimmy Spring
Missed Spring
One Horse Ridge
Perspiration Point

The PCT begins with the infamously dry, hot, beautiful, and sometimes monotonous desert of Southern California, where high temperatures, long dry stretches, and constant battering winds are daily challenges. In the beginning, the trail is packed with "the herd" of hikers all beginning at roughly the same time. For northbound hikers, it is of course the breaking-in period of the trail and full of the struggles of acclimation: physical pain, self-doubt, and loneliness. Occasionally the forested, "sky island" mountains of Southern California offer much needed respite from the desert below, but with new challenges: frigid temperatures, precipitation, and even snow. The extreme differences in elevation, temperature, and environment found between the lower desert and the mountains can be shocking to the uninitiated hiker, many of whom anticipate the desert to be flatter than it actually is. Challenges aside, the wide-open, unhindered desert vistas are stunning, as are the wildflowers, especially after a wet winter.

SONGS STUCK IN MY HEAD

Harry McClintock, "Big Rock Candy Mountain"
Mr. Mister, "Kyrie"
The Tallest Man on Earth, "1904"
Rod Stewart, "Some Guys Have All the Luck"
Willie Nelson, "On the Road Again"
Lauryn Hill, "Doo-Wop (That Thing)"
Linda Ronstadt, "It's So Easy"
King Harvest, "Dancing in the Moonlight"
Phil Collins, "In the Air Tonight"
"Home on the Range"
The Magnetic Fields, "When My Boy Walks Down the Street"
Empire of the Sun, "Walking on a Dream"
"Rudolph the Red-Nosed Reindeer"
Damien Jurado, "Matinee"
Damien Jurado, "Beacon Hill"
Tom Petty, "Crawling Back to You"
TLC, "No Scrubs"
Wings, "Band on the Run"
Wreckx-n-Effect, "Rump Shaker"
Neutral Milk Hotel, "The King of Carrot Flowers, Part One"
Quiet Riot, "Cum on Feel the Noize"
The War on Drugs, "Best Night"
Mark Kozelek and Desertshore, "Hey You Bastards I'm Still Here"
Led Zeppelin, "Tangerine"
Wet Wet Wet, "Love Is All Around"
Iron Train, "Interstate 8"
Mark Kozelek and Jimmy Lavalle, "Gustavo"

REGION

1

MENTAL STRUGGLES

· Constantly trying to avoid poodle-dog bush (a shrub that secretes a severe skin irritant)
· Stressed about resupply logistics, town errands, hitchhiking, alternate routes, and water sources
· Worrying if a missing package will arrive
· Worrying about foot pain and overuse injuries that could end my hike
· Tired of strong, cold winds
· Tired of the desert and Southern California in general
· Self-conscious around large groups
· Insects are a constant annoyance
· Dealing with the temperature extremes in the desert
· Loneliness
· Low morale in the afternoons
· Monotonous terrain and scenery
· General anxiety

NOTES	MONTH	WEATH.	SECTION	MILE	DAY
First river of the trail	🌗	☀️		672.5	32
First view of snowcapped peaks of Southern Sierras	🌗	🌬️		651.3	31
One-quarter of the way to Canada / One month on the trail	🌗	☀️	G	621.9	30 🖼
Scorpion seen	🌗	🌧️		592.9	29
	🌗	☀️		566.5	28
	🌗	🌬️	F		
	🌘	☀️			
	🌘	☀️		517.6	25
Extreme foot pain: worst pain of trail during all-day road walk	🌘	☀️		478.2	24
	🌑	🌬️	E	454.5	23
	🌕	🌬️		444.3	22
Closest point to the Pacific Ocean along the trail	🌕	🌬️			
Pacific Ocean and Los Angeles are visible	🌕	🌨️	D		
First time camping alone since border	🌗	⛅		239.9	12
First rattlesnake seen	🌗	🌬️		218.6	11
Trail name received	🌗	🌬️	C 🖼	197.2	10 🖼
	🌒	☀️		179.4	9
	MAY	🌬️		151.9	8
First coyote seen	🌑	☀️		127.3	7
	🌑	☀️	B	111.4	6
First shower of the trail	🌑	🌨️		91.2	5
	🌘	⛅		68.4	4
				52.6	3
	🌘	☀️	A	32.6	2
				20	1

Kennedy
Meadows
South
⑯

Lake
Isabella
⑮

⑭

Tehachapi
⑬
Mojave

⑫

❶

⑩

Agua Dulce & Hiker Heaven
⑨

Wrightwood

⑧   ⑦

Big Bear Lake

⑥

⑤

Idyllwild

④

Warner Springs   ❸

Julian   ❷

Mount Laguna
❶

Most scenic days
or sections

91

The US/Mexico border | Section A

Sky Islands

The singing heat lay over this desert country, and ahead the stone mountains looked cool and welcoming.

—John Steinbeck, *The Pearl*

Moisture-laden air travels from the Pacific Ocean and gives meaning to the seemingly incongruously named Laguna Mountains, the southernmost mountain range of the Pacific Crest. Even in early summer the Lagunas can be cold and wet and as the hiker climbs, the precipitation can change from rain to sleet and even to snow. With each thousand feet of elevation gained, the temperature drops another five degrees or so. While only forty miles from the border, ecologically speaking up there at nearly six thousand feet, it is as if the hiker has been transported some six hundred miles north.

The slopes are swathed in pine forest, full of trees covered in wolf lichen that glows a bright green. Small icicles descend from these clumps of algae and fungus, and the blue form of a Steller's jay may be spotted amidst the darkened forest. In many other parts of the country it is common to begin a hike in dense forest and climb until above tree line, above that point where conditions are too harsh to support their growth. In the arid landscape of Southern California, however, the tree line is reversed. The lower elevations, so hot and dry, are treeless. It is not until the PCT climbs up into the mountainous "sky islands" of the Lagunas, San Jacintos, San Gabriels, or San Bernardinos that the trees begin to appear. These isolated mountains, so drastically different from the surrounding lowlands, are like forested islands amidst a sea of desert. They can be a refuge from the desert for hikers, but such refuge can often be a double-edged sword, bringing with it the risk of mountain storms or lingering snowpack.

In good weather, hiking through the sky islands can be one of the most peaceful times on the trail in Southern California. In the late afternoon especially, the harsh sun no longer hangs directly overhead but rather peeks over distant ridges and sends shafts of light through the tree cover, while the forest canopy offers shade and respite from the ever-present wind.

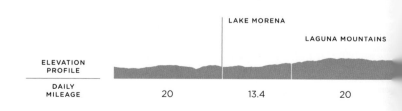

LAKE MORENA

LAGUNA MOUNTAINS

ELEVATION
PROFILE

DAILY
MILEAGE

20   13.4   20

Till the snow ran out in flowers, and
the flowers turned to aloes,
And the aloes sprung to thickets and a
brimming stream ran by;
But the thickets dwined to thorn-scrub,
and the water drained to shallows,
And I dropped again on desert—blasted
earth, and blasting sky. . . .

—Rudyard Kipling, *The Explorer*

The Skookum

The Chinook Jargon—a nineteenth-
century trade language used in the
Pacific Northwest—contained the word
skookum, which was used to refer to a
variety of evil spirits and forest monsters.
While they were sometimes similar to
the Sasquatch, skookums could also be
represented by crows, eagles, owls, blue
jays, and various reptiles. They took on
physical forms but were often described
as malignant entities that could inhabit
people and cause serious illness.

AS HIKERS APPROACH Barrel Springs
the chaparral gives way to taller trees
and from there the trees in turn give
way to large swaths of arid grassland.
Wooden signposts etched with the
letters PCT mark the path for those
times, perhaps in wetter years, when the
grass obscures the trail. The black and
white spots of a group of cows stand
out among the browns, tans, and pale
greens of the landscape. Further along,
on the crest of a small rise stands a giant
stone monolith—the profile of a beaked
head and two massive wings. Eagle Rock

towers above hikers as they pass by on
their way to Warner Springs, backlit by
the sun with outstretched wings, as if it is
descending from the sky upon its prey.

TRAIL NOTES
Warner Springs

A little over one hundred miles in, the
PCT deposited me at a paved road in the
small town of Warner Springs, where the
local community center had opened its
doors to thru-hikers. Burgers and sodas
were available for purchase and hikers
could take a warm shower outdoors
behind the building. As we sat and ate, a
woman entered the community center with her little girl in tow, the child
dressed in a ballerina outfit.

"Can normal people get water here?
Not just people who walked all the way
from Mexico?" she asked gruffly, to no
one in particular.

Outside was an open grassy area
where several large trees provided shade
to camping hikers. Some had been there
for several days, nursing injuries and
waiting to recover before heading back
to a trail more demanding than they had
anticipated. Nearby was a baseball field
with a bathroom for us to use. Behind
it a family of rabbits, with babies small
enough to cup in your hands, crouched
low and trembling in the grass.

In the evening I cowboy camped in
the grass—no tent, just exposed to the
starry sky. The wind began to blow in the
middle of the night and I sat up startled, allowing my inflatable pillow to be
caught by the gusts and blown away into

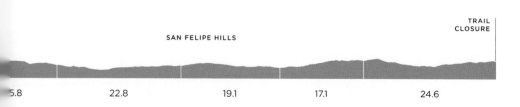

TRAIL
CLOSURE

SAN FELIPE HILLS

5.8   22.8   19.1   17.1   24.6

The San Felipe Hills | Section A

the darkness. I turned on my headlamp and found my pillow trapped between the force of the wind and the chain-link fence that had stopped its flight. I then panned the light across the fence and saw a collection of other hikers' belongings plastered there next to my pillow.

Leaving town via an alternate route, there was a short road walk before coming to Agua Caliente Creek, the first flowing water I had seen so far on the trail. There stood an old adobe church built by the local Cupeño out of wood and earth taken from the nearby hills nearly two centuries ago. The door was unlocked and inside there was a beautiful and quiet ambience about the space. Candles hung on the walls and Easter lilies sat atop the altar. A small bird flew among the hand-split wooden beams and finally settled upon a windowsill next to a statue of the Virgin of Guadalupe and a vase full of daffodils. It began to tap its tiny beak against the windowpane.

Outside a little finch, its head stained a beautiful purple, tapped back from the opposite side of the glass. The chapel is named for Saint Francis of Assisi, patron saint of animals and the natural environment. A fourteenth-century text known as *The Little Flowers of St. Francis* tells of him preaching to a flock of birds so entranced by his voice that they did not fly away. Fittingly, he is often depicted with a bird in his hand.

TRAIL NOTES
The Sky Ranch Sanctuary
North of Warner Springs the PCT reached a dirt road and a sign advertising water, shade, and shelter. I filled my water bottle from a giant metal tank and then descended upon heavily textured stepping stones toward a modest home sitting atop a ridge. It was an off-the-grid complex that belonged to a local trail angel named Mike Herrera. The steps were old grinding stones, traditionally

SAN JACINTOS

SAN BERNARDINOS

18.8   22   21.3   26.1

Eagle Rock | Section A

used to make masa—the corn dough used to make tortillas. In the corner of the yard lying flat in the grass amidst a circle of grinding stones was a marble gravestone dedicated to one Francisco Herrera, who lived from 1886 to 1946. On one end of the gravestone stood a small statue of an American Indian man in full headdress. On the other end was a statue of a woman with long black hair kneeling and patting a pile of masa in her hand.

Not always present at the house, Mike had appointed three caretakers. The first was a man who offered "pack shakedowns," a process by which one hiker helps another, usually a novice, to reduce their pack weight by discarding any extraneous items. He offered a free edible to the first person to shed ten pounds and was aptly named Kushie. The second was a man named Tom who had once opened his own property to hikers until he ultimately had to shutter his operation, succumbing to community complaints and red tape from the county. The third was a man from Seattle who spoke often of his dissociative identity disorder and a host of other health problems. He performed a little charade for everyone present, one which he most likely put on night after night for the captive audience of each new group of hikers.

"Does anyone have a knife?" he asked.

As everyone scrambled to locate pocketknives buried deep in their packs, he wandered over to a nearby wall and pulled down a massive machete.

"Oh, never mind," he chuckled to himself as he sauntered off.

San Jacinto Peak

Straying from the PCT, an alternate route climbs up toward the summit of San Jacinto Peak. It is a trail crowded with day hikers, many of whom arrive via a tram from Palm Springs. Amidst the

SAN GABRIELS

| 24 | 27.4 | 28.6 | 18 | 5 |

Strangest Font Choice on a Trail Sign
Sign north of Warner Springs with a weird 1980s-esque computer font.

jumble of granite boulders at the summit, a view extends out over the Colorado Desert below, including Palm Springs, the Salton Sea, Interstate 10, and the transverse ranges of the San Bernardinos and San Gabriels as they stretch from east to west. From there hikers can see into the future, to where the trail will take them in a few days' time. The view extends from barren desert floor all the way to the snow-covered peak of San Gorgonio—the most drastic change in elevation along the entire route of the PCT. The desert is sporadically carved into grids of civilization, full of greenery otherwise alien to the landscape. Each square of the grid is filled with a different pattern formed by the streets of housing developments. Most are composed of right angles and perpendicular lines, while in a few the neighborhood streets flow and repeat in wavy patterns. On the hills above, wind turbines stand in neat rows like troops awaiting battle.

San Gorgonio Pass

After descending Fuller Ridge, the PCT follows a road and then takes off across a desolate, windswept swath of sandy terrain. There in that narrow passage between two steep mountain ranges, the cool air of the Pacific meets the hot air of the desert interior. The result is a relentless wind that assaults any hiker making their way along the landscape. No trail exists, just tall wooden posts placed intermittently among the paloverde and creosote. When not covered in sand, the desiccated ground is patterned in a network of polygonal shapes. What was once mud has contracted and pulled apart, leaving a delicate array of curved and arching cracks across the ground's surface. This inevitably gives way to more sand. Movement is reduced to slow motion as one passes under the lines of giant transmission towers, plodding along the soft ground while buffeted by the constant winds.

Pine Cones

In the San Bernardinos and San Gabriels, huge mounds of pine cones cluster together in little gullies and depressions, their placement dictated by gravity and the topography of the land. They also trace the contours of the trail by bordering the edge of the PCT on either side, having been inadvertently cleared from the path by an endless parade of hikers. There are larger cones as well. Those

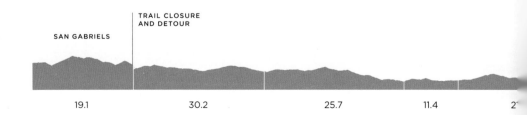

SAN GABRIELS

TRAIL CLOSURE AND DETOUR

19.1   30.2   25.7   11.4   2

of the sugar pine are long and slender, while giant Coulter pine cones are covered in seeds resembling sharp bear claws. It's no wonder they are known colloquially as widow makers—numbered are the days of anyone unlucky enough to have gravity send one hurtling down upon them.

The Angeles Crest

To camp atop the San Gabriels, towering high above the surrounding lowland desert, is to gain a unique perspective. As night falls all of Los Angeles County and the Inland Empire becomes a vast sea of lights lapping at the shores of this mountain retreat. The stars above put on their own stunning show and the moon emerges slowly from behind the trees. The beauty of cowboy camping is waking up throughout the night to notice the heavens changed and to see the moon and constellations glow from a different position each time, as they trace their slow arc across the night sky. Consider yourself fortunate if you need to wake up to relieve yourself in the middle of

Things Found in the 1935 CCC Stone Hut on San Jacinto Peak

The walls of the stone shelter are blackened with soot from fires that once burned in a fireplace long since filled in with rock and mortar. Names have been scraped into the black patina. Various objects crowd the mantle:

- Cowboy hat
- Copy of the New Testament
- Bottle of whiskey (nearly empty)
- Bundle of rope
- Tea candle
- Plastic kazoo
- Cigarette butt
- Two small photos of Thai Buddhist monks

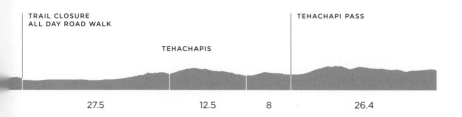

TRAIL CLOSURE
ALL DAY ROAD WALK

TEHACHAPI PASS

TEHACHAPIS

27.5   12.5   8   26.4

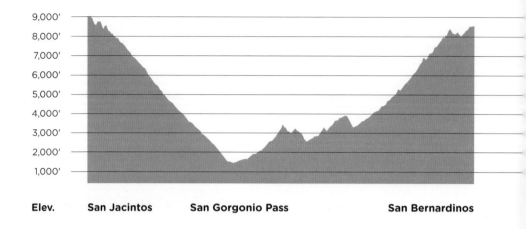

Elev.   San Jacintos   San Gorgonio Pass   San Bernardinos

Most Drastic Change in Elevation on the Entire PCT
62 trail miles

the night, as you wander away from your sleeping bag to gaze out mesmerized at the lights below as they seem to shimmer and dance. While technically amid one of the most populous areas of the United States, one can still find themselves in solitude from atop Saint Gabriel's aerie. Wherever you may be, it's never crowded above five thousand feet.

TRAIL NOTES
Pacifico Mountain

Sometimes a hiker is unlucky and a long, tedious descent occurs at the end of a grueling day, on terrain where a flat spot to camp is simply nonexistent. The dramatic drop from Pacifico Mountain down to Mill Creek Summit was one such descent for me. Several miles into the drop, with the sun nearly gone below

the horizon, I wished desperately to stop and set up camp, but no such opportunity presented itself. I suffered along until finally reaching the covered picnic shelter at the fire station far below.

The following morning brought its own form of drudgery. The day began with a burn area through which the trail was overgrown with toxic poodle-dog bush. Sweat dripped from my brow as the desert warmed and insects filled the air, buzzing around my face and attempting to enter my mouth and nostrils. Charred deadfall and blowdowns obstructed my progress. Climbing over or ducking beneath the seared wood, my clothing and hands became smeared with a charcoal-like residue. I crossed over one blowdown only to immediately crawl beneath another, contorting my

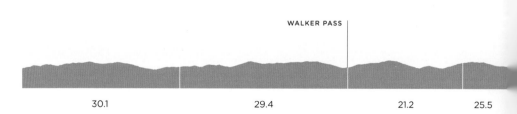

WALKER PASS

30.1   29.4   21.2   25.5

Change in Temperature	Geographical Equivalent in Terms of Plant and Animal Species	Life Zone	Characteristic Plant Species
55°	British Columbia	Arctic-Alpine	Lichen, grass
60°	Northern WA	Hudsonian	Spruce
65°	Southern WA	Canadian	Fir
70°	Southern OR	Transition	Ponderosa pine
75°	Northern CA	Upper Sonoran	Sagebrush, oak
80°	Central CA	Lower Sonoran	Joshua tree, creosote
85°			
90°			
95°			

body in all manner of angles to proceed. I reached a large tree that had fallen across the trail and first penetrated a mass of branches to reach the trunk, which I pulled myself up and over, only to pass through another tangle of branches before exiting on the other side. The trail was heavily eroded, and while traversing a slope, the ground gave way and my right foot slid off the edge, causing me to come crashing down on the other knee.

TRAIL NOTES
Hiker Heaven

With the closing of Hiker Heaven, operated for twenty-two years by trail angels Donna and Jeff Saufley in the desert town of Agua Dulce, an icon of the PCT is in flux. While the property may continue as a business, it will cease to exist as a free space for hikers to stay. I was lucky enough to visit Hiker Heaven during my 2014 thru-hike. At the end of a long road, a PCT logo on a dumpster directed me up a driveway past a corral where horses stood motionless in the heat. Shade tents and cots dotted the property and bales of hay surrounded a large fire pit. A line of porta potties, sauna-like and nearly unbearable in the midday heat, awaited hikers. Volunteers welcomed new arrivals and filled them in on the services offered—the entire operation was a model of organization and efficiency. Hikers could sign up for a shower then exchange their filthy clothing for a loaner outfit. Each hiker's dirty laundry went into a mesh bag to keep it separate from the clothes of others, all laundered in washing machines that

KENNEDY
MEADOWS

4.7

The San Bernardino Mountains as viewed from San Jacinto Peak | Section B

seemed to run continuously without end. Cots were available to sleep on, one of which occupied the shaded area beneath the overhang of a large trailer. Black widows have been spotted crawling on the overhang, a volunteer warned me. There was a large mobile home with a living room, television, kitchen, bathroom, and shower. On the wall hung a framed photograph of a stretch of the PCT somewhere in the Pacific Northwest. The atmospheric forest was foggy and damp and everything the current trail in Southern California was not. I drank in the image and stored it as motivation to get through the last few hundred miles of desert that lay ahead.

Bicycles were available to borrow, and I pedaled into town. Just inside the entrance of the grocery store a large display greeted me. Staples of the typically unhealthy hiker diet—ramen, instant mashed potatoes, and Knorr Pasta Sides—were neatly arranged. A swarm of ten or more hikers arrived, lazily discarded their borrowed bicycles in a disheveled pile, and hurried into the Mexican restaurant. Locals eyed these

hikers descending upon their town like locusts, while business owners profited from their arrival.

From my table in the Mexican restaurant I looked up at black velvet paintings on the walls. One of them depicted men harvesting agave to make tequila. Another illustrated the classic image of the Aztec warrior Popocatepetl, handsome and muscular, hoisting the limp body of his dead love, Iztaccihuatl. The wait staff sang "Happy Birthday" to a little boy. They placed a sombrero atop his head, and he ran about the restaurant singing to himself. Eventually I returned to Hiker Heaven in the dark, feeling bloated and gluttonous as my bike swerved from side to side, grocery bags full of trail food hanging from the ends of the handlebars. I retired to my cot and slept soundly beneath the black widows.

In the morning some hikers prepared to return to the trail, while others chose to linger.

"Are you heading out?" one of the lingering hikers asked me as I strapped on my pack. "Enjoy the heat!" he added sarcastically. I closed the fence door behind me as I left and headed down the driveway, as a dog chased after one of the horses in the corral. The horse grew agitated and kicked up clouds of dust into the air. Some hikers made their way back to the trail by road-walking out of town and others caught a ride to the trailhead. Eventually we all climbed up into the hills surrounding Agua Dulce and continued north.

Casa de Luna

Sadly, along with the Saufleys, another iconic duo of trail angels has recently hung up their hats. After two decades of opening their property to hikers in the small town of Green Valley, Terrie and Joe Anderson's final season was in 2019. Known as Casa de Luna because it typically took hikers a month's time from the border to get there, it had its own distinct atmosphere compared to that of Hiker Heaven. Crowds of hikers gathered in the driveway, smoking, drinking, and conversing. Behind the house a thick forest of twisted, gnarled manzanita seemed at the same time ominous and magical. Narrow paths threaded through the nearly impenetrable woods, leading to secluded campsites. Terrie, matriarch of Casa de Luna, was a warm and generous host and her husband, Joe, was equally friendly. She hugged each new arrival and welcomed them to her home. Everyone was encouraged to put on one of the Hawaiian shirts hanging from a large rack.

As the story goes, Casa de Luna evolved rather organically. Joe had hoped to hike the PCT back in the seventies until a ski injury put an end to his plans. The Andersons moved to Green Valley two decades later, and one random day went to the store while a pot of soup sat cooking on the burner in their kitchen. Joe struck up a conversation

with several PCT hikers who had come into town to resupply. They mentioned they had been craving vegetables.

"Wouldn't you know it," Joe told them, "I have a pot of veggie soup cooking at home as we speak."

He invited them over and thus began an annual tradition of hosting hikers.

Each night Terrie prepared her famous taco salad—layers of tortilla chips, refried beans, rice, beef, tomatoes, olives, jalapeños, and lettuce. Though a more laissez-faire operation than Hiker Heaven, there were still rules. You had to wash your hands first before serving yourself in a strictly prescribed way—all in the interest of keeping things sanitary among a crowd of hikers with generally subpar levels of hygiene. Terrie stood to the side, a wooden ruler in hand, ready to dole out corporal punishment to any transgressors. After dinner hikers gathered and posed for a photo, laughing boisterously as Terrie dropped her pants and mooned everyone, giving new meaning to Casa de Luna.

Things Found or Experienced on a 19.8-Mile Road Walk

- Four of Hearts playing card
- People waving from their cars or homes
- Person with shirt that reads *Welcome to America now learn English or get the fuck out*
- Hiker eating lunch in bushes on the side of the road
- Sign stating that "dogs and ostrich do not mix"
- Sign advertising *Western Martial Arts and Citizen Soldier Training Center*
- Throbbing foot pain
- Popsicle handed from a passing vehicle
- Exotic chickens
- Feral goat
- Pizza and soda offered by a passerby

- Newly hatched chicks belonging to a friendly woman out in her yard
- Motorcycles screaming past
- Drivers blasting their horn just as they are alongside you

Hikertown

Hikertown is located on the fringes of the Mojave Desert near the poppy fields of Antelope Valley and adjacent to the California Aqueduct. It is a ramshackle collection of small buildings, mostly built for novelty's sake, that all add up to a miniaturized fabrication of a Western town. It appears like the stage set of some theater production: a main street lined with various establishments. Post office. Saloon. Jail. Some of the fake buildings are hostel rooms where hikers can stay for the night. When I visited, vehicles were strewn about the property alongside a motley assortment of alpacas, pigs, and dogs. There was a man named Bob who seemed to be the caretaker, with thinning hair that stood up wildly in every direction. He greeted me and noticing that I was left-handed quipped, "Oh, a lefty, eh? Are you ambidextrous? Why, I tell you, I'd give my right hand to be ambidextrous!"

In the midst of that odd Western carnival of the desert, I felt disconnected from my thru-hike. Standing in the door of an old camper that served as my temporary residence, looking out over the broad, windswept plain to the northeast, I felt as if I were in a new home, in a new reality. As if it had always been my home. I prepared dinner in the little kitchenette of an old camper, feeling as if it were already a routine. Beyond the kitchen was a sleeping area with a pillow and sheets that had been last washed who knows when. By the bed was a long horizontal window that framed perfectly the twilit landscape outside. The surrounding mountains were dark silhouettes against a peach-colored sky. In the opposite direction was a horizon full of the blinking red lights of wind turbines off in the distance. Above them the sky transitioned into a clear, star-filled dome. The camper shook periodically from the desert winds. The voice of a woman broke the silence, as she wandered around the property looking for her dog. "Toby? *Tooooby?*" she cried out in a high-pitched voice over and over and over again.

The Skookum

A small group of dead Joshua trees stood nearby my camp, their needles hanging gray and limp toward the ground. Some of them slumped to the side defeated, while others had collapsed completely to the earth. With the sun having long since disappeared behind the hills, their appearance, in tandem with the biting wind, gave that secluded little valley a forlorn and ominous feel. As the stars slowly revealed themselves, their brightness seemed to add a bit of life to the otherwise somber atmosphere. Night completely fell, and a small V-shaped notch in the surrounding hills revealed a framed vista extending out over the flat desert floor to the east and the far-off shimmering lights of civilization.

As I hiked along the next morning, the revolving shadow of a wind turbine's blades fell directly across the trail and with each turn I nearly flinched, the shadows playing tricks on me. In my weary mind those shadows had materialized into a swiftly moving three-dimensional object that with each rotation threatened to slice directly through my legs. The windmills had become Don Quixote's giants and unlike that Spanish knight-errant I had little energy to fight against them. I had spent all morning "tilting at windmills" as I psychologically battled the desert wind, and I had nothing left to give.

The Mojave Desert

In the 1970s *National Geographic* wrote that the officers of the Tejon Ranch Company, which owned more than 270,000 acres of the Tehachapi Mountains area at the time, were negotiating with the Forest Service on a right-of-way across the ranch, which is one of the largest pieces of private property in California. Four decades later that easement for the PCT is yet to be established and therefore thru-hikers find themselves hiking across the floor of the Mojave Desert rather than up in the cooler mountains. Someday thru-hikers will be able to roam the Tehachapis, the last known breeding grounds of the California jaguar before it was extirpated. They will gaze out at Antelope Valley, famous for its brilliant orange poppies, where pronghorns once roamed before they too disappeared.

The waters of the Los Angeles Aqueduct flow along to the left, withheld by sloping concrete banks. The trail then makes a ninety-degree turn and the water disappears underground and into a pipeline that flows parallel to the PCT. The trail itself follows a perfectly straight dirt road that leads off to the horizon. Other hikers appear as minuscule specks in the distance. Their forms stand in stark contrast to the sandy ribbon of road but are soon shrouded in a cloud of dust kicked up by a truck heading south down the road. Ahead of them the road eventually disappears from sight and olive-colored mountains rise up from the horizon to dwarf their tiny figures below. Joshua trees grow in abundance

Rorschach Test
Should a hiker be lucky enough to shower or do laundry, they may notice when removing their shirt that the back of it is stained dark with sweat. Lines of salt deposits trace contours where their pack and its straps have been, all amounting to what looks like the patterns of a Rorschach test.

along the right side of the trail. Oddly, to the left, there is not a single tree. Old, discarded tires sit at odd angles on the ground below them. A couch and numerous trash bags lay scattered about. A bright yellow sign rises crooked from the earth, mostly covered in rust and riddled with bullet holes; its declaration of *No Trespassing* is barely legible. A flock of sheep spreads out across the trail, bleating in odd tones and staring blankly at hikers as they block passage along the trail. A distraught hiker sits forlorn on the side of the trail, tending to his battered feet and counting the number of missing toenails.

TRAIL NOTES
Mojave

Mojave was a windswept, economically depressed desert town situated along a noisy highway, comprised mostly of gas stations and fast-food restaurants that seemed to remain empty even during lunch and dinnertime. Many of

FEED STORE
CITY HALL

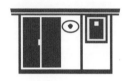

CANTINA
SALOON
CAPTAIN'S QUARTERS

The buildings of Hikertown

the businesses were shuttered, including a McDonald's. Even the most ubiquitous of chain restaurants had given up on Mojave. I stopped by the front desk of my motel to purchase a box of laundry detergent and something about my interaction with the man at the counter left a lasting impression. It was for the most part a superficial interaction, but as I matched the attendant's earnest, friendly demeanor with kindness and appreciation I experienced a strong sense of optimism that I had not felt in recent days. There was a sincerity to the man that one rarely feels from complete strangers. Perhaps it was simply the rush of dopamine that came with the novelty of being back in civilization that had ushered in these positive feelings, but it seemed as if there was more to it. Maybe I had entered Mojave with a sense of vulnerability after being so exposed to a harsh, unforgiving landscape and

as a result appreciated the man's kind demeanor all the more.

The following day I noticed a message on a wooden church sign that read "God Opposes the Proud and Gives Grace to the Humble." Though not particularly religious, I felt drawn to this statement. I realized that what I had sensed in the motel employee was humility, and it was a humility I too possessed after the road walks, harsh winds, and pain of the previous section of trail. Humility, rather than pride, I imagined, must be the prevailing disposition of anyone living in such a windswept town and unforgiving landscape. Pride is reserved for those who drive through Mojave on Highway 14 en route to more luxurious and hospitable locales, perhaps sneering from behind a windshield at such an unassuming little spot in the desert. I may have easily been one of those people under different circumstances,

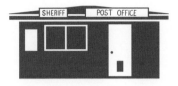

SHERIFF AND POST OFFICE

HOTEL

GUN SHOP

JAIL

BARBER SHOP

DOCTOR'S OFFICE

but instead I had walked there across the land and felt grateful for the comforts Mojave provided, no matter how modest they were. It is the land, after all, that is the origin of humility. The Latin *humus* refers to the ground, the earth, and the soil. I had arrived in Mojave with a humility bestowed upon me by the very desert ground I had walked upon. It is the earth and dust that humans are born of and will eventually return to. The desert, whether we like it or not, quite effectively reminds us of this fact.

And by now he was an expert tramp, using humility as a working principle. He was lean and sun-darkened, and he could withdraw his own personality until he made no stir of anger or jealousy.

—John Steinbeck, *East of Eden*

EACH TIME I OPENED the door of my motel room to the outside world I was greeted by an abrasive environment of blinding sunlight, blasting wind, and blaring train horns. I was reminded of that scene in the movie *Beetlejuice* when Alec Baldwin and Geena Davis open the door to exit their home, only to enter the harsh desert landscape of an alien world, populated by giant worms that burrow through the sand.

In the evening I braved the gusting winds to go purchase trail food at the grocery store. My shopping finished, I exited the store with four paper bags full of groceries, all devoid of handles. Cradled in my left arm I held three bags stacked on top of each other with a fourth grasped tightly in my right. Halfway between the store and the motel the top bag toppled over, dumping its contents across the pavement. As soon as the bag emptied, it was picked up by a gust of wind and disappeared into the night before it had even touched the ground.

Pro Tip Bring your empty backpack (you know—that thing you've been carrying all your belongings in for the past month and a half?) with you to the store and easily and comfortably carry your groceries back to your motel room.

Twenty-Mule Team

Borax is a component of many detergents and cosmetics, and in its early days the town of Mojave was the terminus for the famous twenty-mule teams that carried loads of borax from Death Valley. It was brought across the Mojave Desert to be shipped by rail out of the small desert town. Stephen Mather, an American industrialist and conservationist, made millions in the sale of borax and later became the first director of the National Park Service. In Washington's North Cascades, PCT hikers pass through the Stephen Mather Wilderness, named in honor of Mather in 1988.

Southern California Is Difficult

· Wind
· Heat
· Lack of shade
· Dry stretches
· Pack weighed down with water
· Dusty trail
· Difficult hitchhiking
· Crowded
· Lack of wilderness

The Skookum

As I traveled through the Mojave I could hear what sounded like a conspiracy of ravens. They remained out of sight but filled the desert air with an eerie cacophony, sounding more like snarling animals than birds.

I stopped often to rest and gaze out over a far-off mountain range. Its lower half was obscured by a layer of haze, leaving only its highest peaks to form a ridge of dark serrations that seemed to hover disconnected over the horizon. Between the Tehachapis, where I stood, and those distant mountains the desert was an open plain dotted with small knolls of earth that resembled black, rotting teeth. The dark shapes of ravens sat atop the Joshua trees and watched me as I passed by.

The First River

Just south of Kennedy Meadows a wall of riparian greenery rises from a deep gully. At this point thru-hikers are close to reaching the South Fork of the Kern River, but know that after nearly seven hundred miles, the PCT can be deceptive. It may likely be another mile of twisting and turning trail before actually reaching the river. But then there is a bright flash of light—the sun shimmering on the river's surface. It is cause for celebration, but it is soon followed by a desperate laugh as hikers realize a thick tangle of vegetation separates them from the water's edge. The trail continues through a desertlike landscape, paralleling the green barrier.

Worst Typography on a PCT Trail Sign
All-caps use of Brush Script on the Bird Spring Pass sign.

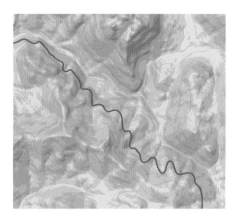

Southern California's Never Ending Side Canyons

It is an all-too-typical feature of the PCT in Southern California: the trail dips deeply into a side canyon—the cleft of a sloped hillside—traces its contour, eventually making a 180-degree turn and then heads back out. From that point a hiker may spot another hiker rounding a similar bend on an adjacent ridge. "I'll catch up in no time," the hiker may think. As the crow flies, the two hikers are quite close, but it is an illusion of the trail. Before reaching that point, which looks so very close, the trail must first dip in and out of the next side canyon. And so it continues on repeat: in and out and around a bend. In and out and around a bend. Each time you round a corner you hope for something different, only to be met with a view nearly indistinguishable from the last. Hiking the PCT in Southern California can often feel like pure drudgery. Two of the worst areas for this are before the descent to Soledad Canyon Road south of Agua Dulce and before reaching Rockhouse Basin just south of Kennedy Meadows.

TRAIL NOTES
The End of the Desert

I stopped at a small bluff that looked out over the river below. I spread out my ground sheet and sleeping bag on the bare rock as night fell and the stars gradually appeared. Lying on my back I watched the blinking lights of a plane passing overhead. The aches and pains of my feet, oddly subdued while hiking throughout the day, now screamed out for attention. A few mosquitoes buzzed through the air but soon disappeared along with the fading light. Above, bats flew in erratic paths, their shapes barely discernible against the dark backdrop. In contrast, shooting stars sporadically traced graceful arcs over the black vault of sky. To be there on the cusp of the Sierras, I felt an excitement that I had never quite felt before. Would these next few weeks be the best of the entire trail? Or perhaps the Sierras would prove to be more mentally and physically brutal than the desert. At that moment, it hardly mattered. Simply existing on the brink of it, with all its uncertainty, was pure exhilaration.

Kennedy Meadows South

Perhaps the most iconic feature of the Kennedy Meadows General Store is its large deck full of hikers all engaged in mainly the same pursuit—consuming as much food and/or beer as possible while sorting through the new supplies they will soon be carrying on their backs for a week or more into the High Sierra. They sit there wondering how they can possibly fit seven days' worth of food into a bear canister that only holds about four and a half. Hikers typically start a tab and settle up before heading out into the South Sierra Wilderness, perhaps a little dazed and bewildered by just how much money one can spend in a twenty-four-hour period in the middle of nowhere. Between breakfast and lunch a hiker may purchase a pint of Ben & Jerry's ice cream, sit out on the deck and look at

it skeptically, wondering, "Can I really finish this off in one sitting?" Ten minutes later it will inevitably sit empty on the table in front of them—a situation bound to repeat itself many more times along the trail.

TRAIL NOTES
Kennedy Meadows Cross-Cultural Communication

I overheard a Japanese hiker in the general store attempting to pay for his dinner. He gave his name (which meant nothing to the woman behind the counter) and told her what he had ordered: a "single burger." With his thick accent, however, the woman had no idea what he wished to communicate. She gave him a long, blank stare punctuated finally with an emotionless, "*Ummm . . . what?*" I thought about stepping in and helping but remembered how annoyed I would get when living in Japan and Japanese people would treat me as if I couldn't navigate day-to-day life on my own, so quick to jump in and assist the "helpless" foreigner. So I left Mr. Cup (his trail name) to fend for himself. There would be many more small towns to come along the trail and many

more interactions like that ahead of him. Each time, I imagined, he would get a little more adept at navigating his way through them. I respected him not only for the courage to take on a challenge such as the PCT, but to pile on top of that the struggles of communication in a foreign language. It was difficult enough at times, when you felt physically and mentally exhausted, to have patience in fulfilling your basic desires for food or a shower. Taking away the ability to clearly communicate seemed to me like the potential final push toward a mental breakdown.

Next to me on the deck, a few locals asked a British thru-hiker where he was from.

"I'm from the UK," the man replied.

"Northern UK?" a young woman inquired after taking in his accent.

"That's right!" the hiker answered, somewhat surprised.

"Liverpool, by chance?"

"Yes! How did you know?"

"Yeah, I watch a lot of BBC . . ."

I witnessed a language barrier even among Canadians and Americans, as one Canadian hiker spoke with an American woman well known in the trail community.

"You're really doing a lot to help out the PCT, *eh?*" he said in classic Canadian parlance.

"The PCTA [Pacific Crest Trail Association]?" she asked, misinterpreting him. "No, I haven't worked with them before . . ."

Steinbeck &
California Toponyms

In his novel *East of Eden,* Steinbeck writes about the toponyms of California and how they originated. He mentions the Spanish explorers, explaining that they were religious people and that the men who could read and write were the priests who traveled with the soldiers. Therefore the first names of places were saints' names, such as San Bernardo or San Francisquito.

Religious holidays also provided some places with names:

Natividad the Nativity
Nacimento the Birth
Soledad the Solitude

Places were also named from the way the expedition felt at the time:

Buena Esperanza good hope
Buena Vista because the view was beautiful
Chualar because it was pretty

The descriptive names followed:

Paso de los Robles because of the oak trees
Los Laureles for the laurels
Tularcitos because of the reeds in the swamp
Salinas for the alkali that was white as salt

Then places were named for animals and birds:

Gavilanes for the hawks that flew in those mountains
Topo for the mole
Los Gatos for the wild cats

The suggestions sometimes came from the nature of the place itself:

Tassajara a cup and saucer
Laguna Seca a dry lake
Corral de Tierra for a fence of earth
Paraiso because it was like Heaven

Eventually, he writes, the names of places refer to events that happened there, and to Steinbeck these are the most interesting, because each name suggests a forgotten story:

Bolsa Nueva a new purse
Moro Cojo, a lame Moor (Who was he and how did he get there? Steinbeck wonders)
Wild Horse Canyon, Mustang Grade, and **Shirt Tail Canyon**

The names of places carry a charge of the people who named them, reverent or irreverent, descriptive, either poetic or disparaging. You can name anything San Lorenzo, but Shirt Tail Canyon or the Lame Moor is something quite different.

—John Steinbeck, *East of Eden*

In the Sierras there are two little mountains which were called by the early settlers 'Maggie's Bubs.' This name was satisfactory and descriptive, but it seemed vulgar to later and more delicate lovers of nature, who tried to change the name a number of times and failing, in usage at least, finally surrendered and called them "The Maggies," explaining that it was an Indian name.

—John Steinbeck, *The Log from the Sea of Cortez*

Central
CALIFORNIA
THE SIERRA NEVADA

We went on our way into the
wonderland of nature gone nuts. . . .

JOHN STEINBECK
Travels with Charley

**FAVORITE
TOPONYMS**

Big Dry Meadow
Chicken Spring Lake
Cloud's Rest
Consultation Lake
Cup Lake
Dutch John Flat
Flat Note Lake
Forgotten Canyon

Hellhole Lake
Jigsaw Pass
Knapsack Pass
Lake of the Lone
 Indian
Last Chance Meadow
Poison Meadow
Saucer Lake

Sharp Note Lake
Shooting Star
 Meadow
Siberian Pass
Starkweather Lake
Thunder and
 Lightning Lake

Everything seems to change after Kennedy Meadows. Water is abundant. Your feet are less dirty. The desert is behind you. The incomprehensible beauty of the High Sierra lies ahead. All of this comes at a price, of course, as the thru-hiker once again has to acclimate to a new environment. The high altitude, snow travel, creek crossings, and daily routine of going up and over a high mountain pass are tests of both mental and physical resiliency. The days are exhausting and the pace can slow significantly. In Southern California and at other points along the trail, the thru-hiker covers sections that perhaps only a thru-hiker would wish to trek. In Central California, on the other hand, thru-hikers find themselves on a trail that nearly every hiker on earth dreams of experiencing. North of Yosemite National Park, the crowds thin out and the terrain becomes somewhat easier and less dramatic, but no less beautiful. The mornings are less frigid, yellow mule's ears cover the grassy slopes, and hikers pass alongside Lake Tahoe—the largest alpine lake in North America.

MENTAL STRUGGLES

- Stressed about my pack weight, resupply logistics, town errands, expenses, and hitchhiking
- Doubtful about my ability to get through the Sierras and complete a thru-hike
- Worried about life after I finish the trail

SONGS STUCK IN MY HEAD

The Who, "Baba O'Riley"
Talking Heads, "Burning Down the House"
Genesis, "That's All"
The Cure, "Just Like Heaven"
Oasis, "Wonderwall"
Kurt Vile, "Wakin' on a Pretty Day"
Smashmouth, "All Star"
The Magnetic Fields, "Reno Dakota"
The Magnetic Fields, "The Death of Ferdinand de Saussure"
Bryan Adams, "(Everything I Do) I Do It for You"
Bill Withers, "Use Me"
Ja'net Dubois, "Movin' on Up"
"Meet the Flintstones"
Nirvana, "Come as You Are"
Simon and Garfunkel, "The 59th Street Bridge Song (Feelin' Groovy)"
AC/DC, "Back in Black"
Tom Jones, "It's Not Unusual"
Weezer, "El Scorcho"
Blink 182, "All the Small Things"

NOTES	MONTH	WEATH.	SECTION	MILE	DAY
Grouse attack	🌑	rain	L		
	🌑	sun		1139	62
Only the second time camping alone on the trail	🌘	sun		1113	61
Began hiking alone for the first time in nearly six hundred miles	🌗	sun	K	1092.9	59
Lake Tahoe first seen	🌗	sun		1080.1	58
Summer Solstice (Hike Naked Day), no nudity witnessed	🌓	sun		1050.2	57
	🌓	sun		1027.8	56
Second bear sighting	🌔	wind			
Bear canister sent home			J		
Second bird nest found sitting on the trail	🌕	wind		1001.4	54 ◼
One-thousand-mile mark					
	🌕	wind		976	53
	🌕	sun		954	52
Socks and shoes smell horribly bad					
	🌕	wind		932.1	51
Trail most crowded since Southern California	🌕	sun	I	914	50
First shower in eight days	🌖	storm		896	48
Trout seen swimming upstream					
Boat ride on Lake Edison	🌗	sun		874.5	47
Coyotes heard at night					
Bird nest found sitting on the trail	🌘	sun		870	46
First bear seen					
First freezing cold creek crossing: South Fork of the Kings River	🌗	cloud		847	45 ◼
Best reflection of the PCT: Fin Dome in Rae Lakes	🌗	cloud		827.5	44
First shower in eleven days				809	43
Most uncomfortable night on the trail	🌗	sun		793.5	42
First snowfields and postholing					
First creek crossing: Rock Creek	JUNE	sun			
First backcountry lake of the PCT: Chicken Spring Lake			H ◼	778.7	38 ◼
Last sagebrush of the trail	🌑	wind		747	36
Last cactus of the trail	🌑	sun			
First marmots seen					
Bear canister picked up					

112

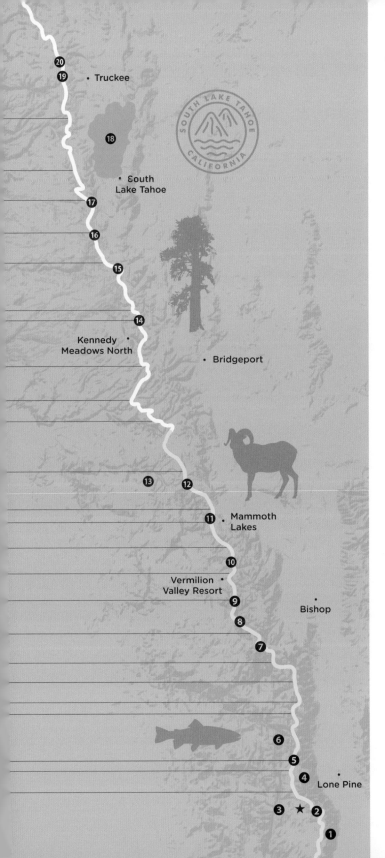

Truckee

• South
Lake Tahoe

Kennedy •
Meadows North

• Bridgeport

Mammoth
Lakes

Vermilion •
Valley Resort

Bishop

Lone Pine

LANDMARKS

Peter Grubb Hut, 20

Donner Pass, 19

Lake Tahoe, 18

Echo Summit, 17

Carson Pass, 16

Ebbetts Pass, 15

Sonora Pass, 14

Yosemite National Park, 13

Donohue Pass, 12

Reds Meadow and
Devils Postpile
National Monument, 11

Silver Pass, 10

Bear Creek,
infamous creek ford, 9

Evolution Creek,
infamous creek ford, 8

Muir Pass, 7

Kings Canyon
National Park, 6

Forester Pass, 5

Mount Whitney, 4

Sequoia National Park, 3

Cottonwood Pass, 2

Olancha Peak,
southernmost peak of the
Sierras that is above tree
line, 1

Most scenic days
or sections

Longest roadless
stretch of the PCT
238 miles

★
Celebrity Sighting Halfmile,
creator of the map set used
by many thru-hikers

113

The South Sierra Wilderness | Section G

South Fork of the Kern River

In the South Sierra Wilderness the PCT skirts along sprawling Monache Meadow and then rounds a bend, crests a small rise, and drops to the South Fork of the Kern River. The sun shines brightly in a large blue sky and the temperature is mild and comfortable. A lazy, shallow river flows beneath a graceful bridge. Swallow nests cling to the underside of its arch and their occupants flit in and out. Blackbirds stride through the shallows looking for food. The river's banks are grassy and verdant. For once, the thru-hiker may resist the urge to press on.

Foxtail Pines

Throughout the Southern Sierras the snags of foxtail pine trees stand amongst massive boulders, the grain of their trunks dramatically spiraling round and round from base to tip. They look as twisted and contorted as a dish rag wrung dry. In some cases, all that remains is a stump. The rest of the tree has long since fallen and disappeared, leaving what looks like a twisting cyclone of wood rising from the ground. The trunk shoots up like a helix, its spirals of wood ending in thin and jagged fingers, tendrils reaching up toward the sky. They appear as if they have been frozen in mid-formation as they corkscrew up from the earth on their way to forming a tree—more a tree being birthed than the remains of one long since dead.

Mount Whitney

Hiking the PCT north, the Sierras spread out for miles to the left, gradually descending toward the San Joaquin Valley. To the right they drop off dramatically, careening down to the arid

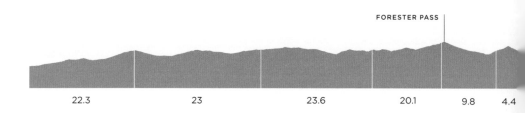

FORESTER PASS

| 22.3 | 23 | 23.6 | 20.1 | 9.8 | 4.4 |

South Fork Kern River | Section G

lowlands lying east of the crest. Nothing illustrates this geology better to a thru-hiker than the popular side trail that ascends Mount Whitney, the tallest peak in the contiguous United States.

En route to Guitar Lake, the setting sun casts dramatic shadows across the surrounding mountains. One ridge casts its shadow upon an adjacent one, dividing it into night and day, like the light side of the moon and the dark. The sunlight slowly changes to golden hues of yellow, orange, and peach. Ridge tops appear as if they are on fire and their image reflects in small streams that in turn flow like molten glass through the meadows. Darkness eventually covers the landscape and tiny pricks of light pierce the inky backdrop, their movement barely perceptible as they inch along the trail far above—the headlamps of hikers making their way up Whitney.

After only a few hours of sleep a group of thru-hikers rouse and pack up in the pitch black. As they climb, the temperature plummets into the low twenties. The wind seems to blow without end. Without a headlamp they'd be unable to see their hands in front of their faces. Their noses drip continually; gusts of wind picking up the snot and carrying it through the air. What doesn't blow off into the wind drips down onto their lips, which become raw and chapped. The world is reduced to the small circle of light emitting from a headlamp. Only the snow at their feet is visible and beyond that everything disappears into a black void. At times they lose their momentum and in turn their balance, nearly toppling over. All they can think of is reaching the shelter at the summit, entering and closing the door—shutting out the wind and cold and darkness of night.

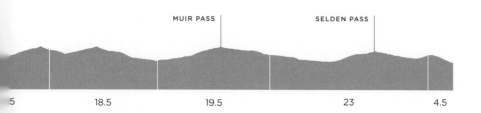

MUIR PASS

SELDEN PASS

5   18.5   19.5   23   4.5

West   **The Sierra Nevada Escarpment**   **East**

Western Biotic Zones		Eastern Biotic Zones
	11,500'	Alpine Zone
Alpine Zone	10,500'	Subalpine Forest
Subalpine Forest	9,000'	Upper Montane Forest
Upper Montane Forest	7,000'	Lower Montane Forest
Mid-Montane Forest	4,000'	Pinyon-Juniper Woodland Zone
Lower Montane Forest	3,000'	Sagebrush Scrub Zone
Lower Woodland and Chaparral Zone	1,000'	Saltbush Scrub Zone

Soon they sense they are making their way up a broad and open summit and eventually see the silhouette of the shelter ahead. They climb the last few yards toward the building and fling the door open only to find four other hikers, with all their gear, already packed into the tiny space. They slump down against the frigid stone wall, wedged between the others.

Time passes and the subtle glow of morning light shines through the tiny window above. Finally, they are able to watch the sun rise from 14,505 feet. Across the landscape only the tallest peaks and ridges glint in the first light. The rest of the landscape remains in darkness, shadowed by the giant escarpment of the eastern Sierras. Frozen lakes sit lonely in high basins. Sunlight slowly flows across the summit and the roof of the shelter. The rocks seem to glow with warmth, though the air is still as frigid as it had been in the dead of night. A sense of calm and comfort washes over the hikers as a result of the shining sun. It is as if they had somehow doubted the sun would ever rise and feel utterly relieved that something as certain as the break of day has actually occurred.

They stand there staring dumbfounded at the sea of peaks until there is nothing else to do but head back down. The climb up Whitney, being an out-and-back detour off the PCT, is a unique experience for thru-hikers, who

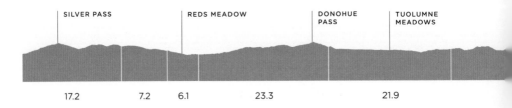

SILVER PASS   REDS MEADOW   DONOHUE PASS   TUOLUMNE MEADOWS

17.2   7.2   6.1   23.3   21.9

typically never retrace their steps. In the daylight everything is now visible. Giant spires of rock rise to the left and then drop straight down. They seem to be one edge of a massive fissure that has formed in the earth, as if the mountains have cracked and split and the other edge lay thousands of feet below. There are gaps between those large spires, like windows opening out on to the eastern horizon and the desert far below. When first passed by in the predawn blackness, their existence unknown, the lights of Lone Pine had seemed to magically appear, only to inexplicably vanish into the night a few steps later.

Forester Pass

There is a long snowfield, pockmarked with the footsteps of previous hikers. Forester Pass looms above, sitting in the apex of a large V-shaped notch in a gargantuan rock wall that seems as if it would impede any northward progress. It is like a great barrier erected long ago, cutting one off from the forbidden kingdom beyond that snowy wasteland— the canyon belonging to the Kings River, originally named El Río de los Santos Reyes (the River of the Holy Kings).

Snowy switchbacks lead up to the highest point along the PCT. The trail crosses over an icy couloir, twists a few more times, and then reaches the top of the pass and the warmth of the sun. To the south is Sequoia National Park where a large expanse of land is bisected by the jagged shadow cast from the ridge to the east. To the left of that saw-toothed contour night remains. To the right, the snowfields shine brightly in the day's first light. To the north is Kings Canyon National Park. Another immense snow-field sprawls across the terrain and plummets down toward an icy lake. Waves of mountains unfold as far as the eye can see. Each new view usurps the previous as the most beautiful scenery of the trail thus far.

Lone Pine

One of the best places to eat breakfast along the entire PCT is the Alabama Hills Café and Bakery, so named for the nearby rock formations that served as the setting of many an old television and film Western. The hills themselves were named by prospectors in honor of the Confederate warship CSS *Alabama*. The mountain pass many hikers cross over to depart the Sierras and reach Lone Pine was named for the USS *Kearsarge*— which sunk the Alabama—by prospectors with allegiances to the North.

The owner of the café is a talkative man in a cowboy hat who holds court over his restaurant from behind the counter and speaks loudly of fishing and the Los Angeles Aqueduct, which originates in the nearby lowlands east of the Sierras. The water is channeled from the Mono Lake basin all the way to Los Angeles using only the force of gravity. Thru-hikers walk above that flowing water as they cross the Mojave Desert. The Owens Valley has been completely sucked dry by the Angelenos, all its potential for agriculture long since

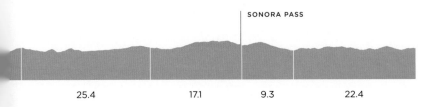

SONORA PASS

25.4   17.1   9.3   22.4

Near Palisade Lakes | Section H

A summer evening in Lone Pine brings with it a perfect temperature. From the town, hikers can watch night fall upon the Sierra Nevada as its high crags darken to a silhouette against the burning sky to the west. It is a unique vantage point from which to stare up at the dramatic rise that is the eastern edge of the Sierras, where hikers have just been and where they will soon return. These hikers, recuperating from their first days in the Sierra, will no doubt feel excitement about returning to those mountains and making their way north, struggling up and over high passes, until eventually the Sierras are no more and they find themselves in an entirely new mountain range.

diminished. The white settlers who lost their water inhabited the area for only a sliver of time in comparison to the Paiutes they displaced. The Paiutes have lived there for thousands of years and refer to the land as Payahuunadu, the "place of flowing water." They channeled stream water that had once been snow resting upon High Sierra granite into complex irrigation systems and water-works to bolster the growth of native plants. This all came to an end with the discovery of gold and silver in the area. Ranchers and farmers stole the Paiute irrigation systems and grasslands, until the water was in turn taken by a thirsty city built in a desert far to the southwest.

PCT PTSD

Returning to the desert environment of Lone Pine after being in the alpine beauty of the Sierras.

Glen Pass

Even in a low snow year thru-hikers, still green as far as high-altitude travel goes, may falter in the snow fields leading up to the second major pass of the High Sierra. The altitude begins to take its toll. They must stop often to catch their breath, what becomes a familiar experience during the coming days. Finally, after a few last switchbacks they are up and over the pass and before them is a never-ending mountainous landscape—

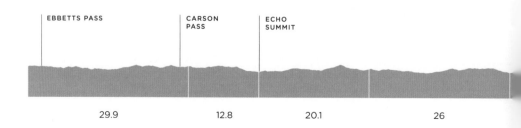

EBBETTS PASS

CARSON PASS

ECHO SUMMIT

29.9   12.8   20.1   26

The trail town of Lone Pine

an endless sea of snowcapped peaks. A steep snowfield leads down toward a granite basin holding Rae Lakes. Numerous small lakes and tarns dot the terrain and run the spectrum between liquid and frozen depending upon their elevation. Heading steeply down from the pass the perspective is dizzying. Hikers feel as if they are on the surface of an icy moon, hovering over a planet below. They posthole with each step, clumsily descending to the valley below, while tiny spiders travel delicately over the snow's surface.

The High Sierra Is Difficult
· High altitude and its effects
· Snowy passes
· Slow travel, covering few miles in a day
· Less frequent resupply points resulting in excess food weight, not to mention the additional weight of a bear canister
· Low energy and fatigue
· The trail is often composed of massive stone steps, difficult to climb up and brutal on the knees when descending
· Cold, dangerous creek crossings
· Wet feet become raw, abraded, and numb due to snow travel
· Postholing in the snow, at times slamming a knee against unseen boulders
· Constant self-doubt

INTERSTATE
80

3.8

Forester Pass	Glen Pass	Pinchot Pass
–	–	–
HIGH PASS	**HIGH PASS**	**HIGH PASS**
№·1	**№·2**	**№·3**
13,153'	11,926'	12,139'
Mile 779.5	Mile 791.1	Mile 807.1

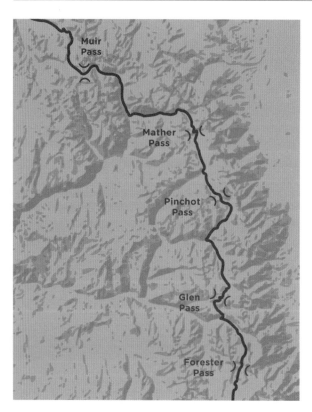

Muir Pass

Mather Pass

Pinchot Pass

Glen Pass

Forester Pass

PASSES
OF THE

HIGH SIERRA

Mather Pass	Muir Pass
–	–
HIGH PASS	**HIGH PASS**
№· 4	**№· 5**
12,067'	11,955'
Mile 816.9	Mile 838.6

Narration from the trailer for the film *High Sierra* (1941)

"This is the highest point in all our land—mighty Mount Whitney. Looming above the wilderness with the strange silence of eternity. Yet stranger still is the mission of destiny that brings men to this forbidding barrier. He's trapped because man can't climb any higher and men never came any tougher. But what brought him here? What made him that way?"

The trail as it switchbacks up to Mather Pass would be all but invisible if not for the way it cuts a zigzagging scar through a snowfield.

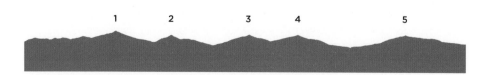

Pinchot Pass

Creeks flow quickly over smooth granite and butterflies fill the air with wings patterned like stained glass. A low, wide pass spreads across the horizon. It is snow-free and looks easily surmountable, but it is not Pinchot. The trail soon curves to the left, disappearing and reappearing multiple times among the snowfields. There are small and infrequent signs of life among the high land of rock and snow and ice. Game trails stretch across a slope to the left, tracing the route of bighorn sheep across the landscape. Frogs croak in small tarns lying below the trail. Huge cumulus clouds brood in the afternoon sky. The trail climbs up steps cut into a giant mound of snow and eventually reaches the pass. From there hikers must head straight down the snowfields, aiming for the distant thread of trail just barely discernable far below.

Mather Pass

On the way to Mather Pass is a gentle climb through beautiful meadow parkland. Deer stand among the sparse trees, alternately foraging and observing hikers cautiously. Climbing into higher, more barren terrain the pass is spotted—a rounded saddle set low between two peaks. Marmots stand on their hind legs and peer out from behind boulders. Camouflaged ptarmigan, clad in brown and white feathers, nearly disappear into the surrounding rock and snow. The trail makes a wide, sweeping curve around the base of the slope then begins climbing up to the pass. The eventual descent down the north side is accomplished mostly by postholing in the snow and when possible using exposed rocks as stepping stones. Further below the melting snow results in abstract formations and swirls of exposed rock twist through the white down toward a frozen tarn.

Mornings in the Sierras

The mornings are cold in the Sierras, and each day I hiked out of camp in the shadows wearing a down jacket, winter hat, and gloves. I moved stiffly through the first few miles until at some point I'd catch a glimpse of a distant ridgeline lit up by the sun. A promise of warmth to come, a rush of excitement came over me. I continued in the shadows until finally, a hundred yards or so ahead, golden light fell across the trail and I knew that I would soon feel it upon my skin.

The valleys were often blanketed in the shadows of early morning and covered in frost. The muddy trail was frozen and a mixture of hard earth and ice crystals. It crunched and cracked with each step. A fallen snag lay across the trail and its broken branches were sheathed in a thin veneer of ice. Further out in the meadow, where the sun's rays had reached, a pair of deer were ablaze in light. Washed out by the sun and standing perfectly still, they resembled marble statues.

Muir Pass

Cresting a small rise, the trail climbs above the tree line into that familiar and severe landscape of rock and snow that heralds the coming of each high pass. Tiny frozen tarns glow an icy blue, like portals into a world of color below the sterile snowfields. Soon enough a pyramidal stone roof comes into view, then a small rock chimney and then the entire beehive form of the Muir Hut. Built by the Sierra Club, its conical form has stood watch over the pass since the 1930s, offering temporary refuge for hikers.

Outside, at nearly twelve thousand feet, the afternoon sun blazes with an unyielding intensity. Soon enough, as if on cue, dark clouds roll in, the wind

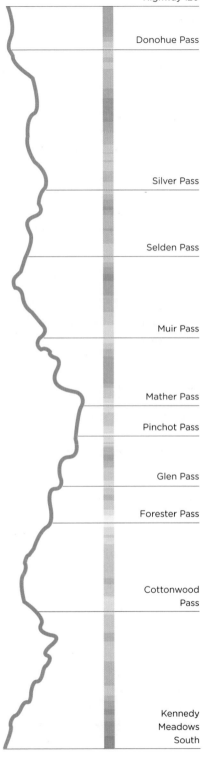

picks up, and it grows uncomfortably cold. Sporadic drops of rain pelt the heads and shoulders of hikers. A familiar descent leads down the north side of the pass, snow and rock under foot. Hidden streams pass below the snow. The PCT travels along the shoreline of a lake, then departs and becomes more of a creek than a pathway. Feet grow soaked and numb. The trail, however, soon leads to Evolution Basin and quite possibly one of the most scenic stretches of the High Sierras. Mounds of granite, bulbous and rounded, seem to bubble up out of the earth's surface. Swaths of bright green meadows sit below lofty peaks and are companions to sprawling alpine lakes. The landscape seems to simply disappear beyond that, as if at the edge of the earth. Unsurprisingly, the trail plunges deep into another canyon.

Selden Pass

The easy ascent of Selden Pass is a far cry from the more dramatic passes to the south. It is a steady climb, but nicely graded with switchbacks and unusually devoid of snow or rocks. The trail climbs to the pass, staying below tree line and passing through a garden of rock and trees, becoming almost labyrinthine at times. Marie Lake, full of islands and peninsulas, sits below. In the slightly overcast afternoon sky the sun shines from behind the clouds, casting a curious light upon everything. The mountains glow in the distance while the lake reflects the

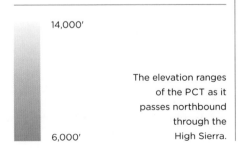

14,000'

The elevation ranges
of the PCT as it
passes northbound
through the
6,000'   High Sierra.

Highway 120

Donohue Pass

Silver Pass

Selden Pass

Muir Pass

Mather Pass

Pinchot Pass

Glen Pass

Forester Pass

Cottonwood
Pass

Kennedy
Meadows
South

The view of Marie Lake from Selden Pass | Section H

clouds above, becoming a steely blue. The wind whips and traces of snow linger on the pass, tucked within the shadows of boulders that shield uninviting bivouac sites. A large group of hikers convenes on top of Selden Pass, nearly all of them identical, clad in long beards and short shorts. A hiker jumps into the frigid waters of the lake below and then bursts to the surface with a loud gasp, nearly hyperventilating from the cold. He clambers to the shore and peers up at the overcast sky, wondering how long it will take to warm up.

TRAIL NOTES
Don't Forget to Look Down

At times in the High Sierra the trail cuts a distinctive line through a meadow. Fringed on both sides by grass, it becomes a deep indentation worn into the ground. I thought of the Scrooge McDuck comics I often read as a child. In them Scrooge had a "worry room" where he paced repetitively in a circle, thinking over his problems and eroding away the floor beneath him. I could remember vividly the way the cartoonist had rendered

that worn pathway and it looked nearly identical to the trail beneath my feet.

The descent from Selden Pass is beautiful and the trail itself appears like inlaid tile.

North of Tuolumne Meadows the trail grows muddy in the damp meadows and hikers become lazy, creating new trails to avoid getting their feet wet. In some places an eyesore of five different parallel trails thread their way through the meadows.

TRAIL NOTES
Bear Creek

At the edge of Bear Creek, one of the Sierra's infamously dangerous fords, I stopped to meticulously place my camera and other electronics into a waterproof bag. As I stood and shouldered my pack, a large group of hikers arrived and plowed into the creek one after the other, barely slowing down. They reached the other side and hiked on with bravado. Alone again, I crossed over and paused at the other side. A straggler from the group appeared, forded the water and emerged onto the shore to ask me, "Was that Bear Creek?"

"That was nothing," he declared with the hubris and unearned confidence of a hiker passing through the Sierras in a low snow year.

TRAIL NOTES
Purple Lake

Alongside another hiker, I stood on the shores of Purple Lake, concerned by the increasing rainfall. The water rippled in the breeze taking on the look of sandpaper. A man hiking by stopped to assuage our fears.

"This isn't a big deal. It's going to rain mostly on the eastern side of the mountains. I've hiked over five hundred days in the Sierras and climbed over one hundred peaks, and I see this all the time. It'll be nothing."

His sentence was punctuated by a blinding flash of lightning. We did not linger to see if his confidence was shaken and immediately began climbing up through tree cover. The rain changed to sleet and then to hail. There were times when the lightning was so close that a flash of bright light was all I could see. It was as if for a split second the world vanished into a void of white and then returned all at once. Adrenaline coursed through me. We hunkered down below a tree and put on our rain gear, thinking we might be able to wait out the storm. It grew colder and we began to shiver.

The wind picked up as we continued to climb, but to my relief we eventually began to drop to the outlet of a lake. We flew downhill along the trail, my body surging with energy and my legs feeling stronger and sturdier than they ever had, negotiating every rock and twist in the trail with ease.

The various elevation ranges of the PCT as it passes through the High Sierra, grouped proportionally.

13,000'
12,000'

11,000'

10,000'

9,000'

8,000'

7,000'
6,000'

Ed the Trolley Driver

My hiking partner and I were the only passengers on the trolley into Mammoth Lakes. Ed, the driver, shouted back at us from his position behind the wheel. It was not a conversation by any means, we were simply two new faces playing our roles as an audience held captive to his storytelling whims. Ed wasted little time, launching into a monologue about his early days running pack mules into the backcountry.

"Backpackers all hate sharing the trail with livestock," he claimed. "As far as I'm concerned, God made horses and mules and if hikers don't like it, they can go to hell!"

His boss at the time, he said, was six feet, eight inches tall and weighed two hundred and eighty pounds. On one sojourn into the wilderness, sitting atop his horse, the boss and a hiker found themselves at an impasse. The hiker had refused to yield the right of way to this behemoth of a man on horseback. The hiker was warned, "Well, if you don't move you might just get kicked."

The hiker assumed he could stay clear of the horse's hind legs and answered defiantly, "I'll take my chances."

The man warned him a second time, "You might get kicked."

Again, the hiker refused to budge.

"Alright," the equestrian said as he began to maneuver his horse around the hiker. Just as they were side by side, the man took his "big, old, size twelve cowboy boot" and kicked the hiker square in the chest.

From there we progressed to a discussion of Ed's run-ins with drunken passengers on his trolley.

"I'm an old man, but if I have trouble with anyone on my bus, I ain't gonna call 911. I'm gonna jump in there and take care of business myself. I might get my ass kicked, but I'll get in the mix! Hell, I'm a former Marine combat veteran. I fought in Vietnam, ran with the Hell's Angels, cowboyed for a living, and I'm one tough son of a bitch!" he explained. "There was this one drunk asshole who had just gone to Pita Pit and brought his pita on the trolley. He was wasted, so I proceeded to kick him off and would you believe it? He took his damn pita and threw it right at me! He missed and I picked the pita up off the ground, chased him down the street, and threw it right back at him. Hit him right in the chest! I said to him, 'Fuck your fuckin' pita pit, you fuckin' fuck!'"

And then Ed transitioned gracefully back into the topic of pack mules, recalling the time he packed out a seasonal park ranger—"the most beautiful woman" he had ever seen. This led him to a discussion about a local woman he was enamored with.

"You can just tell she's a rock climber—her body is so damn beautiful. She works at my favorite breakfast place in town."

Our thru-hiker ears perked up.

"Did you say breakfast place?" I called out to Ed.

Devils Postpile

A short alternate route passes by a volcanic rock formation of columnar basalt named Devils Postpile. Its hexagonal columns tower up toward the sky. For the most part, the vertical stonework seems to rise straight from the ground, but in contrast, on the far left side of the structure the columns are curved and warped and look to have been ripped from their foundation, like a clump of enlarged grass torn from the earth. At the foot of the structure rests a massive

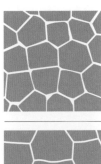
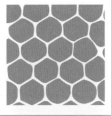

Columnar basalt
Beehive
Salt flat

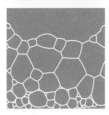

Turtle shell
Soap bubbles
Storm on Saturn

Hexagons found in nature

pile of the six-sided stone pillars, broken into numerous smaller pieces.

The columnar basalt of Devils Postpile. A bee's honeycomb. A snowflake. A layer of bubbles on the surface of water. All of these natural formations share one thing in common—they are hexagonal. In the case of the honeycomb, a tessellation of hexagons is the most efficient way for bees to fill a space using the least amount of raw material possible. In the example of Devils Postpile, during its formation the delicate interplay between cooling and contracting lava, and the resulting tension, necessitated the stabilizing force of the hexagon. A 120-degree angle is apparently the most efficient way to release tension, and the exact measurement of each of those six angles.

Further up the PCT, in Northern Oregon along the popular Eagle Creek alternate route, the trail passes over columnar basalt. It seems to be inlaid with massive hexagonal tiles. Each hexagon varies, some convex and curving upward, others concave and cradling small pools of water.

The Nüümü Poyo: The People's Road

In 2018, members of the group Indigenous Women Hike spent twenty-two days backpacking in the eastern Sierra Nevadas. Under the American Indian Religious Freedom Act they traveled through their ancestral lands without the permits typically required to hike the John Muir Trail, gathering and fishing along the way. The National Park Service was welcoming of their endeavor.

They refer to the trail not as the John Muir Trail but rather "The People's Road," or Nüümü Poyo in the Paiute language. Many different tribal nations use the land and each has their own ways of referring to the mountains and its trails and ancestral trade routes.

TRAIL NOTES
North of Yosemite

I came to a wide, but shallow creek and played what had become a familiar game. I hopped from rock to rock and then reached the final stepping stone, placed just far enough from the oppo-

The Stories Behind Some High Sierra Toponyms

Battle Creek Named for a battle between a burro named Barney and a mountain lion. Barney was the victor.

Bearpaw Meadow Named by early stockmen who found a bear paw nailed to a tree.

Charybdis Along with Scylla, these adjacent peaks resembled the two sea monsters from Homer's *Odyssey*, which guarded either side of a narrow strait.

Devils Postpile Originally named the Devils Woodpile by sheepherders who considered the columnar basalt to be the handiwork of the devil.

Dinkey Creek Named for Dinkey, a little dog that fought a grizzly bear at the creek in 1863.

Evolution Basin Named for Darwin and other evolutionary theory philosophers. Evolution Lake sits below Mount Darwin.

Glen Aulin From the Gaelic phrase for "beautiful valley."

Happy Gap Named for the elation a nineteenth-century prospector would feel upon finally getting a train of pack mules to reach this pass.

Hell for Sure Pass Named for the difficulty of this rough sheep trail.

Hospital Rock A large boulder that was positioned in such a way that it formed a "room," used by the Yokuts as a gathering place and as shelter for sick and newborn babies.

Kings River Named for the biblical three magi. The river has three principal forks.

Merced River Named for the Spanish in honor of the Virgin Mary, El Río de Nuestra Señora (the River of Our Lady of Mercy).

Peter Lake A small lake discovered where a faint trail "petered out."

Reds Meadow Named for "Red" Satcher, a stockman known for his red beard.

Regulation Peak Named for the Yosemite National Park regulations tacked to trees in the area in 1895.

Sardine Lake A mule carrying canned sardines had fallen off the trail and perished in the lake.

Sequoia Named for George Gist, a Cherokee man also known as Sequoyah, who developed an alphabet and writing system for the Cherokee language.

Shuteye Peak Named for Old Shuteye, a one-eyed man who owned a rancheria in the area.

Tunemah Pass Tunemah is supposedly derived from a Chinese expletive, learned by sheepherders from the Chinese cooks that accompanied them in the mountains. It is a reference to the rough and difficult trail that led to the pass.

South of Sonora Pass | Section I

site shore that I began to doubt my ability to make the last leap. I breathed in and used every ounce of energy to spring off the rock and bound toward the shore. Landing squarely on solid ground I involuntarily let out a whoop of exhilaration to echo through the wilderness, with no one else around to hear it. Standing there I watched as two birds of prey in the sky locked their talons and spun downward in tight circles—a dispute over food or territory played out in aerial acrobatics. Still visible in the morning sky, the moon hung large and low just above a tall granite cliff face. I stood for a while and studied their rocky surfaces—one earthbound and the other celestial—and then continued on up the trail.

Worst Typo of the PCT

Signpost south of Sonora Pass that says PTC, rather than PCT.

Sonora Pass

From the top of the climb a long and exposed ridge walk unfurled. Frigid winds blew and the temperature plummeted. My nose dripped constantly, causing my nostrils to crack and burn in pain as if they had been sliced through with a knife. I passed over countless rises, hoping each time that the wind would abate on the other side. I hoped to finally see the highway below but was constantly disappointed. There was only more snow and more talus. It was a miserable and torturous march through an utterly beautiful landscape. Melting snowfields painted abstract shapes across the dark mountains and tiny lake basins reflected the sky to add a welcome measure of color.

Finally I could see the highway down below, curving through green, rounded hills and small pockets of forest. It looked like a completely different world compared to the harsh and barren ridgeline. I stood there feeling relieved and then noticed a trail heading far off to the left, up and over another long ridge. *That can't be the PCT*, I thought. *There must be a junction that I'm not seeing. The PCT* must *head straight down to the road in front of me.*

The junction never came—only more climbing through snowfields, mud, and talus. The road disappeared from view and I simply pushed on. It appeared again and I felt a quick flash of excitement, only to see the PCT curve all the way around a large, open basin—heading nowhere near the highway. My shoes were full of rocks and I began to sweat—the gloves and layers of clothing I needed on the ridge walk were no longer necessary as I descended—but I couldn't bring myself to stop and remove them. The only thing I could do was propel myself around the endless twists and turns on my way to the road. It would have to show itself eventually.

Kennedy Meadows North

Behind the lodge at Kennedy Meadows, a resort and pack station west of Sonora Pass, is a low ridge of rock and trees that catches the last light of the day. In front is a meadow bordered by a wooden fence and a small manmade stream. An older man who strikes the figure of a fairly convincing cowboy walks by, followed by his young grandson, who twirls a lasso. The boy releases the rope, attempting to snare his grandfather's feet. The older man feigns tripping, stutter-steps, and continues on without looking back, as if it were a game they had played many times before. A pair of butterflies rises straight up in the air, all the while spiraling one around the other. They twirl up higher and higher as the sun shines through their translucent wings and then finally separate from their synchronized dance and flutter off. In the saloon a jukebox plays the gunfighter ballads and trail songs of Marty Robbins, his voice filling the bar as he sings about the old West Texas town of El Paso.

Ask a Thru-Hiker
I sat in the resort's lobby waiting to eat breakfast. "Did you pass through the Colorado Desert?" a man asked, referring to a section of the Sonoran Desert in Southern California. Before I could answer him, another man interrupted. "*Ummm*, Colorado? That's like four states away, dude."

I wondered what had become of Darren, the British hiker with whom I hitched into town. It turned out he had left at five a.m. to return to the trail. He began at the Mexico border long after me and had not taken a single zero day. He was relentless and too fast it seemed even to receive a trail name. When asked why he was hiking the PCT, he answered simply, "It sure beats working."

Irony on the PCT
Spotting a bear near your camp the very same day you have mailed your bear canister home.

Eldorado

As the day comes to a close the setting sun casts a beautiful, golden light on the fractured peaks north of Sonora Pass until they become like the citadels of a lost city of gold. Fittingly, from there it is only a few days north to the boundary of Eldorado National Forest.

Most Creatively Named Toponyms That Are Adjacent
Talking Mountain and Echo Lake

Approaching Lake Tahoe | Section J

The Desolate Impossibility

North of Lake Aloha, in the Desolation Wilderness, a hiker watches a plane fly low overhead. It is quite close and thus its velocity seems all the more apparent. It travels north in the same direction as the trail and makes it painfully obvious just how slow the hiker is traveling on foot. The state of California, not to mention the entire PCT, seems so unfathomably long when taken one step at a time. As Steinbeck expressed as he drove his looping route around the country in *Travels with Charley*, "Suddenly the United States became huge beyond belief and impossible ever to cross. I wondered how in hell I'd got myself mixed up in a project that couldn't be carried out. It was like starting to write a novel. When I face the desolate impossibility of writing five hundred pages a sick sense of failure falls on me and I know I can never do it. This happens every time. Then gradually I write one page then another. One day's work is all I can permit myself to contemplate and I eliminate the possibility of ever finishing."

Steinbeck's explanation encapsulates the thru-hiker's desired mentality. When viewed in totality the PCT is an impossible endeavor, therefore it must be approached in more manageable doses. One must contemplate only the prospect of reaching the next town. The hiker cannot consider the "desolate impossibility" of reaching Canada so many hundreds of miles north of where they currently stand in the Desolation Wilderness. Bear in mind that Canada lies north along a route not as the crow flies, but rather along the twisting, snaking, and sometimes maddening route of the PCT as it traces the spine of the Pacific Crest, up and over high passes and down into valleys and even as low as sea level at the Columbia River. It turns west and east and yes, sometimes even south, as it slowly leads the hiker to Monument 78 at the Canadian border.

NORTHERN CALIFORNIA

THE KLAMATHS & CASCADES

It is very strange that when you set a goal for yourself, it is hard not to hold toward it even if it is inconvenient and not even desirable.

JOHN STEINBECK
Travels with Charley

FAVORITE TOPONYMS

Alcohol Jacks Reservoir
Bloody Run Trail
Butcherknife Creek
Cayenne Ridge
Devils Half Acre
Devils Oven Lake

Doodlebug Gulch
Firstwater Creek
Goodbye Lake
Hello Lake
Humbug Summit
Jackass Spring
Man Eaten Lake

Milkhouse Flat
Mumbo Basin
Music Creek
No-See-Um Camp
Shanghai Creek
Slaughter House Flat
Tangle Blue Lake

As the Sierra Nevada comes to a close, thru-hikers must prepare for yet another test of mental endurance. The intense heat, tree cover, logging areas, and general lack of scenery can be a tough transition after the incomparable Sierras. Dramatic granite peaks rising high above tree line are a thing of the past. One often hikes in tree cover and when views do appear, they are simply of low, forested mountains. There are long, steep descents into tiny trail towns followed by long, steep climbs back out. Hikers celebrate the midpoint of the PCT as the trail enters the Cascade Range. The trail soon makes a dramatic westward turn to avoid the inhospitable terrain to the north, but not before passing over the hot and dry Hat Creek Rim. Both the days and the nights can be sweltering. Luckily there is the beauty of Lassen Volcanic National Park and the ever-present Mount Shasta to keep hikers going until they reach the incredibly wild and scenic Klamath Mountains.

SONGS STUCK IN MY HEAD

Kansas, "Dust in the Wind"
Bachman-Turner Overdrive, "Takin' Care of Business"
Rusted Root, "Send Me on My Way"
David Bowie, "Young Americans"
Chuck Berry, "You Never Can Tell"
"James Bond Theme"
Mase, "Feel So Good"
2Pac, "I Get Around"
Digital Underground, "Humpty Dance"
Creedence Clearwater Revival, "Susie Q"
Sun Kil Moon, "Heron Blue"
Foghat, "Slow Ride"
Bon Jovi, "Livin' On a Prayer"
A Tribe Called Quest, "Electric Relaxation"
The Penguins, "Earth Angel"
Wilco, "Bull Black Nova"
Echo and the Bunnymen, "My Kingdom"
U2, "Mysterious Ways"
Ugly Casanova, "Barnacles"
Coldplay, "Clocks"
Elvis Presley, "Hound Dog"
Little Richard, "Good Golly, Miss Molly"
The Pointer Sisters, "I'm So Excited"
The Beach Boys, "Help Me, Rhonda"
The Four Seasons, "Sherry"
Beck, "Strange Apparition"
Blue Oyster Cult, "(Don't Fear) the Reaper"
Hot Pockets jingle
George of the Jungle theme song

MENTAL STRUGGLES

- Stressed about how much food I should carry out of town
- Stressed about hitchhiking
- Stressed about issues back home in Seattle
- Stressed about digital voice recorder breaking and having to order a new one
- After a zero day, unmotivated to return to the trail amid mediocre scenery and intense heat
- Tired and burnt out

NOTES	MONTH	WEATH.	SECTION	MILE	DAY
The most I perspired on the trail: the climb out of Seiad Valley in triple-digit heat	◑	🌧	R		
Westernmost point on the PCT	○	☀		1630.1	84
	○	☀			
	○	☀	Q	1606.5	83
	○	☀		1571.1	81
Longest the trail travels southbound (for a northbound hiker)	○	☀		1542.4	80 🖼
Cowbells first heard on the trail, a common sound in Northern California	○	⛅	P 🖼	1515.3	79
Catch foot on a root and fall flat on my chest	○	☀		1476	76
One of the hottest nights on the trail	○	☀	O	1423.5	74
Third bear sighting of the trail, came face-to-face with a bear					
Bear prints spotted on the trail	○	☀			
Cougar prints spotted on the trail					
	◖	☀		1394.9	73 🖼
Mount Shasta first seen	◖	☀			
	◖	☀		1373.6	72 🖼
	◐	☀			
	◐	☀		1344.1	71
	◑	☀		1318	70
Lassen Peak first seen					
One of the hardest climbs of the trail	JULY	☀	N	1289.5	69
Start of the Cascade Range End of the Sierra Nevada	◕	☀			
Copy of John Steinbeck's *Cannery Row* added to my pack	●	☀		1250.9	67
First shower in nine days					
Banana slug seen	●	☀		1226	66
Most thru-hikers seen since Southern California					
	●	☀		1194.8	65
	●	🌧	M	1192.8	64

134

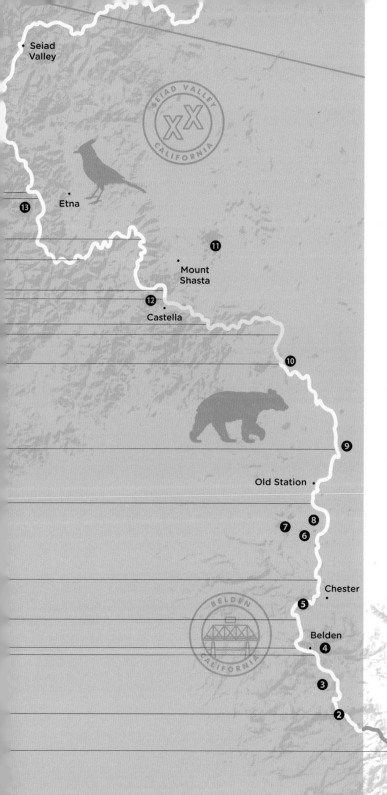

Seiad Valley

Etna

 13

11

Mount Shasta

12 **Castella**

10

9

Old Station

7 8
   6

Chester
5

Belden
4

3

2

1 → **Sierra City**

LANDMARKS

Marble Mountains, 13

Castle Crags State Park, 12

Mount Shasta, 11

McArthur-Burney Falls
Memorial State Park, 10

Hat Creek Rim 9

Lassen National Park, 8

Lassen Peak, 7

Drakesbad Guest Ranch, 6

PCT midpoint, 5

Little Haven, trail angels, 4

Bucks Lake, 3

Swimming hole,
Middle Fork of the
Feather River, 2

Sierra Buttes, 1

Most scenic days
or sections

Least enjoyable part
of the trail: Section O

135

Peter Grubb Hut

Outside the rain continued to fall and fog slowly spilled into the meadow. A small peak above became completely socked in. I lay in my sleeping bag atop the wooden floor of the loft, staring out of the small window as the light faded and the trees became dark shapes against the sky. The floor shook and vibrated every time someone walked across it. You could count the number of shelters along the PCT on one hand and perhaps the number of times it rains on the trail in California on the other, and yet somehow there I was—lucky to be under a roof as the world soaked outside.

Ask a Thru-Hiker Special Installment: People Don't Know What Trekking Poles Are

Leaving Donner Pass I met a man who stared down at my trekking poles. "Is there snow up in the mountains?" he asked, most likely confusing them with ski poles. "What the hell are you doing up there—just hiking?" A few days later another man saw my poles and yelled out to me, "You're too late for snow!"

"Did you catch any fish up there?" a man had asked me back in Southern California.

I couldn't fathom why anyone would ask such a question in the desert. I could only assume he mistook my trekking poles for fishing poles.

"Can't say that I have," I replied.

Sierra City

A log cabin with a red tin roof stands along a dirt road on the outskirts of town. Ivy grows up its tall stone chimney and huge sugar pine cones have been strung along the eave of the front porch, while clothing hangs in the yard to dry. Turning onto Route 49, hikers soon enter the small hamlet of Sierra City, only a few blocks long and lined with quaint homes and shuttered businesses. In the early morning it is silent and empty, without a person in sight. Red, white, and blue bunting adorns many of the buildings in anticipation of Independence Day. The rugged peaks of the Sierra Buttes rise high above it all.

Three backpacks sit neatly in a row in front of the Red Moose, a hiker-friendly restaurant and inn. Thru-hikers sit inside eating eggs and pancakes and drinking coffee. Behind the building they've pitched their tents on a grassy lawn perched high above the North Yuba River, looking out on a view of low, forested mountains—a view that will soon become familiar to them in Northern California. Lit up by the morning sun, the trees are as light and delicate as feathers, the hills resembling some great bird covered in evergreen plumage.

Hikers walk down the still deserted street and wait for the store to open so they can buy trail food, do laundry, and sit out on the front porch doing what thru-hikers do best when not hiking—consuming calories. With each passing hour, more hikers slowly funnel into Sierra City. A hip, young couple enters

SIERRA CITY

30   3   28.5   24.9

the store, passing through town on a road trip. The woman is dressed in a vintage 1950s style, with white-blonde hair and horn-rimmed glasses. The man's affectation reads more blue-collar. Despite the summer heat, he wears a flannel shirt, stiff denim jeans, and a matching denim jacket. A pair of leather work boots finishes off the look. A rag hangs from his back pocket, as if at any moment he might change someone's oil or dab the sweat from his brow. A local teenager sizes them up from behind the counter, then leans toward the man working next to him.

"Is that how you dressed when you were young?" he teases.

"Shit, I ain't that old!" his coworker shoots back.

Fun Fact Google Street View captured a front porch full of thru-hikers at Sierra City's Sierra Country Store in July 2015.

Ordering a Beer in Sierra City
The proprietor approaches and a hiker asks if he has anything on draft.

"Nope," the man answers.

"Okay, how about bottled beer?"

"Yep, we got bottles."

"*Umm*, okay. What do you have? Any local beers?"

"Ain't nothing local," he replies.
The hiker settles on a beer from Reno.

Annoying Graffiti of the PCT Between Sierra City and Belden
Written in marker on five consecutive metal blazes:

Pea See Tea
Dehydration is your worst enemy
Welcome to Dogwood Heights luxury camp
Bury your TP, you DB
DB = douchebag

TRAIL NOTES
Feather River
A large steel bridge arched over the Feather River below. I looked down at the water, disappointed to see no one swimming. In typical fashion I had arrived to camp much later than the others. I dropped my pack and headed immediately for the water, first wading through the river on slippery rocks and then making my way down a narrow pathway along the opposite bank, which led me to the most perfect of swimming holes. I stripped off my clothes and plunged into the water. It felt euphoric floating there as I caught the last rays of sunlight before they disappeared behind the canyon wall. I hadn't showered in over a week. As I floated I noticed what looked to be a stick in the water before me. Much to my surprise it was a small water snake, swimming briskly with its tiny head breaking the surface of the river. It passed directly by me with a sense of urgency, as if wary of me and simply hoping to make it by unharmed. It was comical, one moment alone and the next making direct eye contact with a snake.

The day was going fast now. Only the tops of the Gabilan Mountains flamed with the light of the sun that had gone

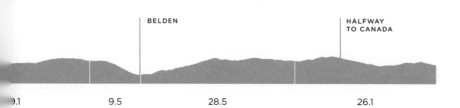

BELDEN

HALFWAY TO CANADA

.1   9.5   28.5   26.1

from the valley. A water snake slipped along on the pool, its head held up like a little periscope.

—John Steinbeck, *Of Mice and Men*

Belden

I finished the steep descent into Belden and stepped over a dead milk snake on the trail, its body twisted into contortions of red, black, and white stripes. The colors of the snake's skin echoed the colors of the resort below—the reds and dark blues and whites of its buildings, steel bridge, and faux totem poles. Belden Town Resort, found directly along the PCT, possesses a stunning location on the North Fork of the Feather River. Tree-covered peaks rise up above the river canyon and an old, red steel bridge is adorned with a long-defunct neon sign depicting a cocktail glass. Inside the bar/restaurant, a long table full of hikers shouted at a TV broadcasting the World Cup. The table was covered in trash—the detritus of everyone's breakfast. Out the window a northbound hiker on the other side of the river began the long climb back up into the mountains—a view into the near future for the group of hikers gathered around that table.

The bar is decorated with old beer cans and vintage slot machines. The mounted heads of a moose, wildebeest, and wild boar stare out unblinking from the walls. In an unattended store, inflatable rafts and pool toys hang from shelves in packaging faded from the sun.

In the restroom, a thru-hiker was shaving his head at the sink. Hikers can pay to wash their clothes in a laundry room where every surface is covered in a thick layer of dust. They can then shower in a derelict bath house with a shower stall covered in multiple layers of chipped and peeling paint that obscures any underlying filth. An older man loitered outside, while a hiker complained of having to walk around in the triple-digit heat in his rain gear as he washed his only pair of clothes.

"Just walk around naked. That's what everybody does at the festivals," he said, alluding to the infamous raves held there on the weekends.

From Belden Town Resort, hikers can arrange a ride to the home of the Braatens, who own an adjacent cabin where hikers may stay. A tiny stream flows through their property and a rooster and a few hens can often be seen wandering about pecking at the ground. There is a small bird bath in the yard—a statue of Saint Francis of Assisi with birds resting on his arms. During the day, the interior of the cabin can be unbearably hot, making the swimming hole directly across the highway a welcome reprieve. Hikers repeatedly alternate between the cool river and the sun baked rocks along its shore.

The Skookum

I hiked along as butterflies floated lazily through the air above me. Out of nowhere a grouse shot past my head and began to flutter in tight loops around me.

HAT CREEK
RIM

27.7   21.3   28.6

The bridge leading to Belden Town Resort, spanning the North Fork Feather River | Section N

It would buzz past me from one side, compose itself, and then swoop down on me from the opposite angle, letting out a series of clicking noises all the while. It was disorienting, as I spun around trying to keep my eyes on the bird, hearing it more than actually seeing it. Eventually it retreated from its attack, alighting upon a tree branch where it chirped in agitation as I passed on.

Sunset

Atop a dry ridge north of Belden the sun slowly drops and spreads its orange glow across the landscape. A hummingbird zips past, the buzzing of its wings clearly audible. It shoots by multiple times—back and forth, back and forth. It drops into the grass to reach a flower and then instantly reappears as it propels itself straight up into the air, hovers in place for a moment, then shoots off parallel to the ground and out of sight.

The sun drops lower and lower, fading from orange to red. A distant mountain range that had remained invisible during the haze of the late afternoon begins to slowly materialize on the horizon as the sunset deepens. Just before the sun disappears it seems to grow into a fiery inferno. From atop the ridge a hiker looks out at a large area of burned forest and feels as if he has solved some great mystery. The land had not been

INTERSTATE 5

30.9   30.5   8.8

A view of Mount Shasta from Hat Creek Rim | Section N

set ablaze by a wildfire, but rather each night it is scorched by the setting sun. The moon hangs in the sky above, small and crescent-shaped. It is beautiful yet unable to hold its own against the sun's final show of the day.

Midpoint

In the midst of a less than scenic section of forested trail stands a diminutive concrete post marking the halfway point between Mexico and Canada. Inscribed upon it in a crude typeface is *PCT mid-point*, with every letter in *midpoint* set in lowercase as if to remind thru-hikers that the glass is only half full, and the trail is only half conquered.

Tipping the Scales

North of the trail's midpoint, hikers may detect a noticeable mental shift. The scales have been tipped and with each step more trail lay behind than ahead. The desert and the Sierras feel like such singular and iconic experiences. They demand all of the hiker's attention, and it's hard to look beyond them and con-sider the rest of the trail. Now, however,

the hiker finally, truly feels in the midst of a thru-hike. With the less dramatic terrain and oftentimes lackluster scenery of Northern California, it becomes simply about the slow progression north along the trail. The day-to-day act of walking is what matters most, rather than reaching any specific destination. In thru-hiking there is a simplicity to daily goals and the overall objective. Just ticking off miles and literally moving forward makes every day feel like an accomplishment and with half of the trail completed, confidence soars.

How the Bumpass Hell Area in Lassen Volcanic National Park Got Its Name

Kendall Vanhook Bumpass was a settler and cowboy who worked in the Lassen area in the late nineteenth century. While showing the area to a local newspaper editor he broke through the ground above a boiling mud pot, scalding his leg so badly that it eventually required amputation. The area was henceforth known as Bumpass Hell.

SCOTT MOUNTAIN SUMMIT

27.1   28.7   29.5   5.

Signs at a Gas Station in the Town of Old Station Humorously Threaten Trespassers with Death

· We don't dial 911 around here.
· If you are found here tonight you will be found here tomorrow.
· If you can read this you are in range.
· Violators will be shot. Survivors will be shot again.
· Ammunition is expensive—don't expect any warning shots!

Hat Creek Rim

The plateau of Hat Creek Rim is a notoriously dry and hot section of the PCT—any water that falls on this area drains into the soil and rock and disappears far out of reach. Hikers often plan to cross in the evening or early morning. Like some cruel joke, a wilderness area adjacent to this escarpment is named, of all things, the Thousand Lakes Wilderness. To the south, Lassen Peak stands draped in dramatic shadows, and in the other direction hikers catch their first hazy glimpse of Mount Shasta and its beautiful symmetry. It is the first of the many stratovolcanoes that line the remainder of the PCT, and it will become a constant companion along the trail for days and weeks to come.

A bit further north, hikers can drop down to the campground at McArthur-Burney Falls State Park, along the way stopping to watch the falls, fed by spring water, thunder down into a blue pool. Two main cascades and numerous tiny rivulets create a veil of white that passes over a dripping, green wall of moss and rock. It is a sight to behold in comparison to the dry, scorching plateau of Hat Creek Rim.

Northern California Is Difficult

· Extreme heat and even humidity (it's July after all)
· Long stretches without water
· Dry and dusty trail
· Lack of even a faint breeze
· Lack of views
· Monotonous scenery
· Logging areas
· Lack of wilderness
· Poison oak

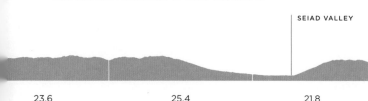

SEIAD VALLEY

23.6   25.4   21.8

The Northern California Blues

North of Lake Tahoe, as the Sierra Nevada comes to an end, hikers may feel a significant drop in morale as the scenery begins to fall short in comparison. They may become discouraged as they realize they are only halfway finished and, in their minds, the climax of the PCT is already behind them.

The forests are no longer beautiful. They are crowded only with tall trees. Hungry for the sun's rays, they seem to channel all their energy into growing foliage atop the forest canopy. As a result, far below, the forest can appear nearly lifeless, with barren lower branches and no understory of plant life. It is simply the soil of the forest floor and the trunks of the trees, all brown and gray and devoid of any color.

A hiker is positioned in the sun at such an angle that as he hikes along, so too does his shadow beside him. It is not stretched or distorted as a shadow often is, but retains roughly the same proportions as the physical body. The hiker looks over at his shadow's arms as they pump back and forth, trekking poles in each hand. *This is all I do for nearly twelve hours a day,* he thinks. *I make that same motion as I move constantly north along the trail.* It is an odd sensation, as if he has stepped outside of his body for a moment to look at his experience objectively and reduce it to its most simplistic and uninspiring form.

North of the PCT midpoint, the trail continues through the trees, alternating between National Forest land and privately maintained logging areas. Occasionally there is a break in the tree cover and hikers are exposed to the scorching sun. Large clouds of dust rise into the air. It is perhaps the first taste of just how hot Northern California can get in the height of summer and a harbinger of things to come. The tree cover and heat of Northern California can prove quite the mental obstacle for the thru-hiker. As Steinbeck observed, "How can one know color in perpetual green, and what good is warmth without cold to give it sweetness?"

A Matter of Perspective
The Sound of Aspen in the Sierras, Where Water Is Abundant and the Days Are Cool Aspen leaves shimmer in the light and fill the air with a beautiful music, as if instead of leaves the branches were adorned with thousands of paper-thin castanets.

| CREEPING SNOWBERRY | MILKVETCH/ LOCOWEED | STICKY CINQUEFOIL | AMERICAN TRAIL PLANT |

The Sound of Aspen in Northern California Where Water Is Scarce and the Days Are Unbearably Hot Aspen leaves shake in some imperceptible wind that the hiker's skin cannot feel. To the ear, they make a cruel sound like flowing water, taunting the thirsty.

Obligatory John Muir Quote

I watched a Steller's jay make its way up a tall snag. With a hop and a flutter of its wings it moved from branch to branch, climbing higher up each rung of its makeshift ladder. I had always found the Steller's jay, with its darkly crested head that gradates into a brilliantly blue body, to be an incredibly beautiful, albeit obnoxious bird. As any piece of writing about nature or hiking seems to quote John Muir, I too shall favor tradition. I will include, however, not an inspiring quote about the mountains, but rather one that echoes my own disdain toward the sound of the Steller's jay. In *The Yosemite,* Muir writes, "The Steller's jays were, of course, making more noise and stir than all the other birds combined; ever coming and going with loud bluster, screaming as if each had a lump of melting sludge in his throat."

You Know You Are in the Town of Mount Shasta If You See

· Numerous crystal and gem shops
· A store selling "flower essences for animals"
· A flyer from a house full of Rastafarians reading: "Looking for a likeminded roommate to share good vibes with"
· A large medicine wheel painted on the surface of a parking lot
· A group of young men and women dancing in a circle beside a Volkswagen bus
· Not one, but two, different people wearing a shirt that reads "You mess with me, you mess with the whole damn trailer park" (only one of them may be wearing the shirt ironically)

The Skookum

California folklore tells of the Dark Watchers, humanoid figures often seen standing motionless atop the mountain ridges of the Santa Lucias. They silently observe passing hikers below. The entities appear to be giants, sometimes as tall as fifteen feet, often black silhouettes that seem to be clad in dark robes, brimmed hats, and walking staffs. The Chumash knew them as the Old Ones and early Spanish explorers called them Los Vigilantes Oscuros. Encounters continue to this day, with witnesses sometimes first observing a large black raven or condor, before a more humanoid figure begins to materialize. Steinbeck wrote of the Dark Watchers in his short story *Flight*. In it the watchers are silent observers and leave passersby alone, so long as the humans stay to the trail and show no interest.

THIMBLEBERRY

WILD GINGER

SIERRA GOOSEBERRY

CALIFORNIA SPIKENARD

A vintage Coca-Cola sign in the town of Castella

In California's Russian Wilderness, as hikers make a long climb along the PCT near Russian and Grizzly Peaks, there stands a granite sentinel atop the ridge to the north. The Statue, as it is known, is a humanoid shape, though of gigantic proportions, with a clearly defined head, broad shoulders, and sloping arms. Its head is crowned with a conical shape not unlike that of a hat. It stands watch over the ridges and river valleys, guarding small Statue Lake, which rests in a beautiful granite cirque over the ridge behind it. The Statue watches hikers as they pass directly below, most likely unaware of the lake that remains just out of sight. It is best to continue on toward Etna Summit and show no interest in the watcher and its treasure.

The State of Jefferson

As the PCT begins to turn northeast out of the Klamath Mountains and veer back toward the Cascades, it passes through the heart of the State of Jefferson. This region of rural Northern California and Southern Oregon had first proposed its secession in the 1940s, but the movement lost steam as World War II began and all attention shifted to the war effort. The people felt little connection to the more populous areas of California and Oregon and considered themselves underrepresented in state government. On the wooden post of a PCT trail sign just before Seiad Valley someone has carved "State of Jefferson" alongside two large Xs—the "double cross" logo illustrating the belief that the region was constantly slighted by the governments in Salem and Sacramento. The economy of the State of Jefferson has long been inextricably linked to natural resource extraction. So with the proposal for expansion of the Cascade-Siskiyou National Monument and the conservation

The trail town of Mount Shasta

efforts of the Klamath-Siskiyou Wildlands Center (KS Wild), old wounds had been opened. What one side saw as protection of an area with unprecedented biodiversity, the other side saw as a federal "land grab" which would result in restricting access to public lands and a threat to their livelihood. When passing through the area, PCT hikers in 2014 passed sign after sign proclaiming "No Monument" and "KS Wild Lies."

TRAIL NOTES
Seiad Valley

On the front porch of a home sat two women. They waved and called out to me as I passed by, "Good morning! You're only a mile from the store!" From there the trail continued, following a road that curves south and then north again, then east, before finally shifting west toward town where it crosses the Klamath River on a steel bridge. Seiad Valley consists

of little more than a fire station, post office, store, and café. On the wall of the café hangs faded Polaroids. In them, PCT hikers smile widely at the camera. They are all victors in the café's pancake challenge, in which one must consume five thirteen-inch-diameter pancakes within a two-hour time limit—nearly nine pounds in total. I passed time in the adjacent general store, wondering if I had missed my window to tackle the infamous climb out of town before the day grew too hot. I signed the trail register—there's been one at the store since the early days of the PCT. The man behind the counter mentioned that the hottest part of the day is between three and seven p.m. I wondered aloud if I should spend the day in town or head back to the trail immediately. "There's one thing that never changes," he says. "The mountain is always going to be there. It will still be there tomorrow morning. And really, it isn't all that bad. I've been up there to hunt and I'm old and fat and didn't hike here from Mexico."

I left town as quietly and anonymously as I had entered and soon saw a sign for the PCT. Crossing the road I found myself back on trail and steeply climbing. The temperature reached triple digits and my body was almost immediately drenched in perspiration. My clothing grew dark as it soaked up the dampness. I reached Fern Spring where cool water flows from a pipe into a concrete trough. The sound of the dripping water filled my ears. I placed my bottle below the thin stream and instantly the sound ceased and the forest fell into silence. It was only me and my thoughts and the little black water bugs that milled about inside the trough. Then I pulled back my bottle and the sound of water once again filled the air.

TRAIL NOTES
The Pines
One evening north of Seiad Valley I ate dinner and then lay in my bug net reading *Cannery Row*. Resting on my back, I held the book aloft, opened it, and read: "The pines above them soughed in the fresh sea wind. The boys lay in the pine needles and looked up at the lonely sky through the pine branches." I put the book down and found myself staring straight up at the sky through the towering pine trees above me. I smiled at the seamless transition between the book and my own reality.

There, just outside of Seiad Valley, the PCT is at the apex of its long westerly curve, as it swings out widely to avoid the drier lands directly north of Mount Shasta. Though there is no fresh sea wind and it is far from Monterey, as the crow flies those mountains are only forty or so miles from the Pacific. It is the closest to the ocean the trail will pass other than the San Gabriels in Southern California. If the trail continued west one could stand among the coastal redwoods in less than two days' time.

Things Found in a Derelict Cabin Near the California/Oregon Border

A small plastic toy.

Names and initials going back to the sixties carved into the wooden walls and posts.

A photograph of a smiling man. He holds a dog close to him, their faces touching. The photo seems to have been taken within the cabin itself, at a time when it was in better condition. On the photo, written in a child's handwriting, is a message—*I love you and miss you.*

A note written by a thru-hiker two years prior. "Does this long drawn out story have an end? Maybe today, here, now. Bullshit talks and death stalks—the louder I sharpen my killing blade the louder life cries for a second chance. Who am I to decide? Either way, this walk is my last dance. Over, thru and beyond the PCT 2012."

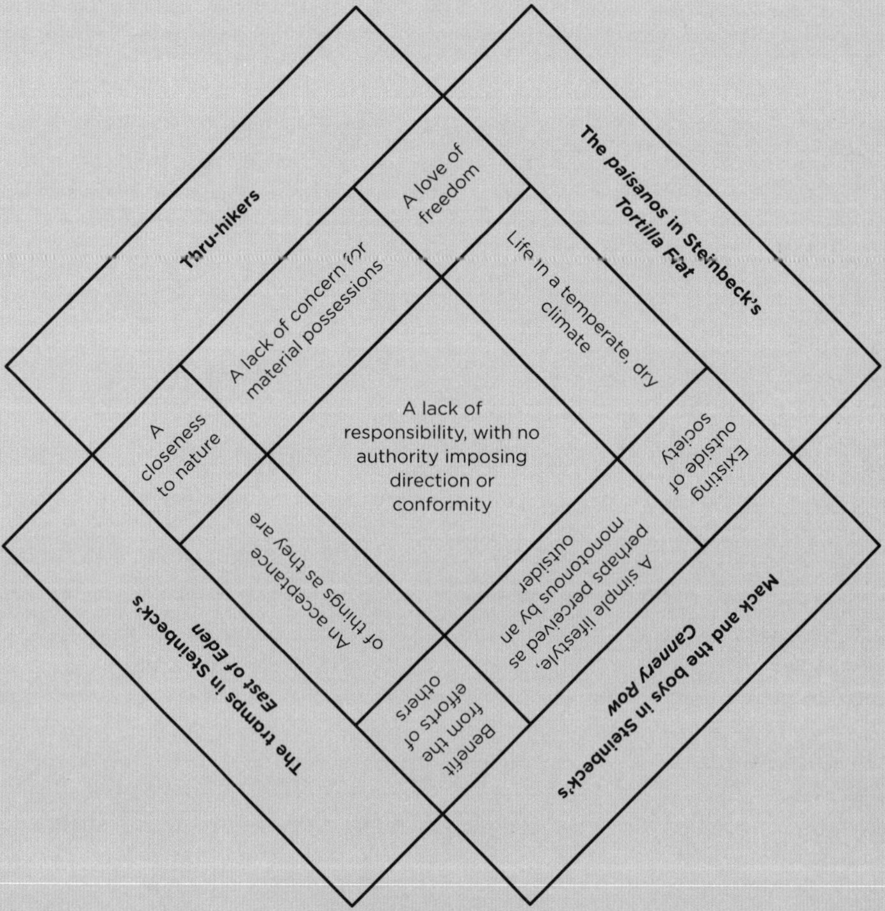
Thru-hikers
The paisanos in Steinbeck's *Tortilla Flat*
The tramps in Steinbeck's *East of Eden*
Mack and the boys in Steinbeck's *Cannery Row*
A love of freedom
A lack of concern for material possessions
Life in a temperate, dry climate
A closeness to nature
A lack of responsibility, with no authority imposing direction or conformity
Existing outside of society
An acceptance of things as they are
A simple lifestyle, perhaps perceived as monotonous by an outsider
Benefit from the efforts of others

Traits Shared by Thru-Hikers and Characters in Steinbeck's Novels

---

I just got into wandering. Couldn't stop.
It gets into you.

Adam Trask in *East of Eden*

15
VIEWS OF
MOUNT
SHASTA

1
July 5, 4:38 p.m.

2
July 5, 7:41 p.m.

6
July 8, 6:35 a.m.

7
July 10, 7:14 p.m.

8
July 12, 9:40 a.m.

12
July 16, 9:28 a.m.

13
July 19, 7:41 p.m.

14
July 20, 10:41 a.m.

Mount Shasta

For almost five hundred miles Mount Shasta is a near-constant companion for the PCT hiker. It towers over the surrounding landscape, a lone sentinel seemingly unconnected to any other major peaks or mountain ranges. This volcano serves as a beacon for hikers during some of the more mentally difficult sections of the trail in Northern California. Shasta is popular as a New Age spiritual location and considered to be a "power center." It is also rumored to contain a hidden city of advanced, white-robed beings from the lost continent of Lemuria.

3
July 6, 4:43 a.m.

4
July 6, 5:23 a.m.

5
July 6, 7:21 a.m.

9
July 12, 10:02 a.m.

10
July 14, 7:36 a.m.

11
July 14, 6:45 p.m.

15
July 25, 6:47 a.m.

First view
From Hat Creek Rim
Final view
From the rim of
Crater Lake
Visible July 5–27
Total days 23

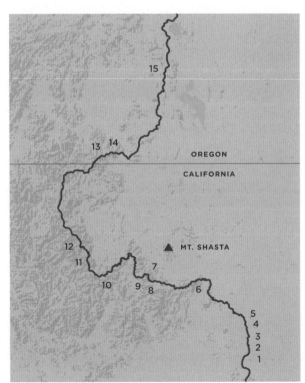

OREGON

THE SOUTHERN CASCADES

A little feeling of hurry was creeping upon us, for by now we had begun to see the magnitude of the job we had undertaken. . . . Our time was going fast.

JOHN STEINBECK
The Log from the Sea of Cortez

FAVORITE TOPONYMS

Devils Pulpit	Jackpot Meadow	Pumice Desert
Dinah-Mo Peak	Nip and Tuck Lakes	Questionmark Lake
Found Lake	Parsnip Lake	Rosary Lake
Four in One Cone	Phantom Ship	The Watchman
Fumarole Bay	Pinhead Buttes	Wildcat Glades
Heavenly Twin Lake	Preachers Peak	Wizard Island
Hidden Lake	Pulpit Rock	

Oregon begins with the dry, brown foothills surrounding Ashland as the trail crosses back over Interstate 5 and ends with the lush forests we typically equate with the Pacific Northwest. The state is best defined by three features. The first is the gentler terrain, which allows thru-hikers to cover quite a bit of ground each day. The second is the string of volcanoes lining the trail, each of them tall, Matterhorn-like spires reaching toward the clouds. The third is the abundance of mosquitoes in July and August when most northbound thru-hikers travel the state. Transitioning between the Klamath Mountains and into the Cascades, hikers may be surprised by the lengthy dry stretches of Southern Oregon, even as they pass the blue waters of one of the highlights of the entire PCT—Crater Lake National Park. Continuing north, much of the trail passes through dense forest dotted with small ponds and lakes. The nights become noticeably cooler and by Northern Oregon all major dry stretches are a thing of the past. The volcanoes of Washington come into view—broader and more rounded in comparison—and hikers can finish out the state on the popular Eagle Creek alternate route. As the trail makes a long descent toward sea level and the Columbia River, it passes an abundance of water making the same journey, spilling down in a variety of incredible waterfalls.

MENTAL STRUGGLES

- Guilt that I am hiking while so many horrible things are going on in the world
- Low morale and low energy
- Extreme thirst that affects mental state
- Questioning the point of thru-hiking
- Lonely and burnt out
- Pessimistic thoughts about life after the trail

SONGS STUCK IN MY HEAD

A Tribe Called Quest, "Scenario"
Patrick Swayze, "She's Like the Wind"
Bob Marley and the Wailers, "Jamming"
Thomas Dolby, "She Blinded Me with Science"
Talking Heads, "Road to Nowhere"
The Rolling Stones, "She's Like a Rainbow"
The Rolling Stones, "2000 Man"
DJ Jazzy Jeff and the Fresh Prince, "Yo Home to Bel-Air
(*The Fresh Prince of Bel-Air* Theme Song)"
The Temptations, "My Girl"
Madonna, "Like a Virgin"

NOTES	MONTH	WEATH.	SECTION	MILE	DAY
First time to sleep under a roof in seventeen days			G	2092.8	104
Worst lack of Leave No Trace principles seen (toilet paper everywhere along Eagle Creek)					
Mount Adams and Mount Saint Helens first seen					
Last sighting of lizards				2057.6	103
Mornings and evenings begin to feel noticeably colder				2030.3	102
First time to hike ten miles before ten a.m.					
First berries of the trail	AUG			2007.4	100
First noticeably difficult climb in Oregon				2001.3	99
One hundred days on the trail			F	1978	98
Mount Jefferson and Mount Hood first seen					
Incredible view of Oregon's volcanoes				1948.1	97
Obsidian on the trail					
Narrowly escape a thunderstorm					
Worst day for mosquitoes on the trail					
Starts to feel less arid and more like the Pacific Northwest			E	1917.8	96
First vintage PCT diamond blaze seen				1884	95
Pack starts to smell noticeably bad				1857	94
Gray jays first seen, a common bird in the Pacific Northwest					
Old-man's beard (lichen) first seen growing on trees			D		
Thirstiest time on the trail					
Mount Shasta last seen				1829.3	93
Two-thirds of the way to Canada			C	1797.9	92
First southbound thru-hiker met					
				1780.3	91
Interstate 5 crossed				1748.6	90
Cougar prints seen on the trail			B	1726.8	88

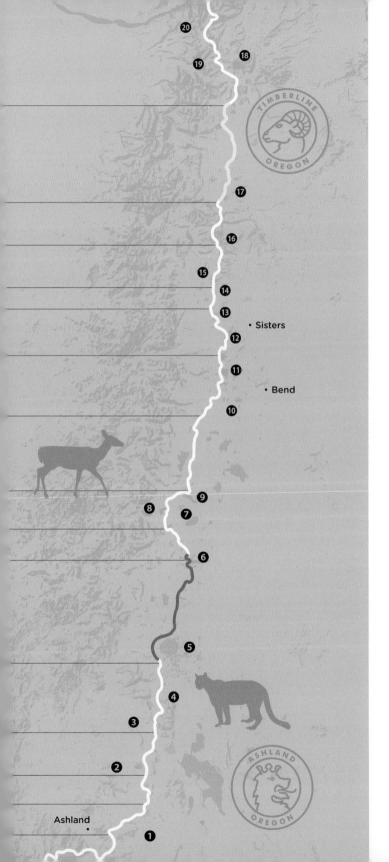

LANDMARKS

Eagle Creek Alternate, 20

Ramona Falls, 19

Mount Hood, 18

Olallie Lake Resort, 17

Mount Jefferson, 16

Three Fingered Jack, 15

Santiam Pass, 14

Mount Washington, 13

McKenzie Pass, 12

Three Sisters, 11

Mount Bachelor, 10

Shelter Cove Resort, 9

Diamond Peak, 8

Oregon Skyline Trail
Alternate, 7

Mount Thielsen, 6

Crater Lake
National Park, 5

Sky Lakes Wilderness
Alternate, 4

Mount McLoughlin, 3

Fish Lake Resort, 2

Hyatt Lake Resort, 1

Most scenic days
or sections

Most miles hiked in a day

Most difficult dry stretch
and thirstiest time on
the trail

Worst day for
mosquitoes

• Sisters

• Bend

Ashland
•

Olallie Lake and Mount Jefferson | Section F

TRAIL NOTES
Reaching Oregon

I tried to look at the landscape and see the beauty of it with fresh eyes, not with eyes that had seen day after day of mountain scenery for over two months. I tried to imagine how it might look on a weekend backpacking trip, after five days spent indoors at a job. What a sight for sore eyes it would have been. I was trying, after walking the length of California, to take nothing for granted.

Racist Names along the Trail That Should Most Definitely Be Changed

Squaw Valley Creek
Darkey Creek Trail
Dead Indian Highway

The Skookum

I camped next to a stagnant pond with views out over low peaks and a parched valley beyond. The Oregon nights were becoming noticeably colder. In all honesty, I had begun to feel burnt out and lonely. I realized that when the nights had been uncomfortably hot, I had been consumed with an underlying edge of frustration, irritation, and perhaps even a touch of anger. The cold, however, seemed to have the opposite effect. As darkness came and I huddled there shivering, I felt a whole host of very different emotions: loneliness, sadness, fear, and humility. I eventually drifted off to sleep and in the night something large passed by my shelter, fallen branches snapping

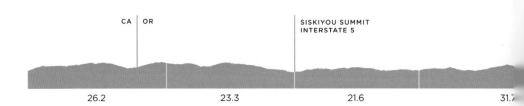

CA | OR

SISKIYOU SUMMIT
INTERSTATE 5

26.2   23.3   21.6   31.7

with each of its steps. Later I awoke to the sound of an animal crying out into the night, as it succumbed to a predator.

The following morning I was woken by a large bird that I heard but never actually saw. The beating of its wings woke me—*whoosh, whoosh, whoosh*—so loud I imagined a wingspan of gargantuan proportions. It landed in a tree above me. After a few moments it broke the silence as it once again flapped its wings. *Whoosh, whoosh, whoosh* and it landed upon a different tree. I began to stir in my tent and it returned to the air once again and disappeared out of earshot. The next morning I was awoken again by a large bird in a tree above me.

The night was cold and aloof, and its warm life was withdrawn, so that it was full of bitter warnings to man that he is alone in the world, and alone among his fellows; that he has no comfort owing him from anywhere.

—John Steinbeck, *Tortilla Flat*

The First View of Crater Lake

1 You see only the crater rim on the opposite side of the lake.
2 Eventually you get to a point where you can see the water.
3 Slightly disappointed, you think, *It's not the brilliant blue color seen in photographs.*
4 Getting closer, you realize you are only seeing the reflection of the rocky rim.

5 You grow elated as you finally see the brilliant blue reflection of the sky in the lake water.

The vast expanse of blue that is Crater Lake sits still and motionless, a perfect and unblemished mirror positioned toward the heavens. Wizard Island rises up from those blue waters, floating in the collapsed caldera of a volcano that erupted thousands of years ago. The island, rising up into a miniature cinder cone, is a perfect addition to an already flawless scene. It sits asymmetrically in the water as a perfect midground focal point, making it nearly impossible to snap a bad photograph of the lake.

Mount Mazama

The eruption of Mount Mazama 7,700 years ago can be thanked for the beauty of Crater Lake. It can also be thanked for the layer of pumice covering the area, which retains very little water from the snow melt. Water drains though the porous earth and disappears beyond the reach of thirsty hikers.

THE LAKE AND ITS NAMES
Original Klamath Name
Giiwas
Various Names Given by White Explorers
Deep Blue Lake
Blue Lake
Lake Majesty
Crater Lake

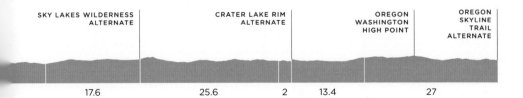

SKY LAKES WILDERNESS ALTERNATE	CRATER LAKE RIM ALTERNATE		OREGON WASHINGTON HIGH POINT	OREGON SKYLINE TRAIL ALTERNATE
17.6	25.6	2	13.4	27

ORIGINAL NAME	Kohm Yah-mah-nee
Corresponding Indian Nation	Mountain Maidu
—	—
VOLCANO	Lassen Peak

| ELEVATION | 10,457' |

The Old Man of the Lake is a thirty-foot hemlock trunk that has been bobbing vertically in Crater Lake since at least 1896. The trunk is around 450 years old.

The Klamath Creation Story of Giiwas

At times, Llao—the spirit of the mountain and Chief of the Below World—would come up from his home inside the earth and stand atop Mount Mazama. On one such occasion he saw the beautiful daughter of the Makalak chief and fell in love. When she refused him, he stood upon the mountain and hurled fire at her people. Skell—the spirit of the sky and Chief of the Above World—stood atop Mount Shasta and defended the people.

The two waged battle from atop their respective mountains, causing fiery landslides and violently shaking the earth. Llao was driven back into Mount Mazama and the mountain collapsed, forming a large crater. Soon a torrential rain began to fall, creating a lake. The Klamath people called it Giiwas. Today it is known as Crater Lake.

Ask a Thru-Hiker

I sat there at Crater Lake with all my belongings surrounding me. My sleeping bag, wet from condensation, lay drying in the morning sun. Crowds of tourists wandered by. A woman stopped and eyed my belongings. "Are you doing that hike-the-trail-thing?" she asked loudly.

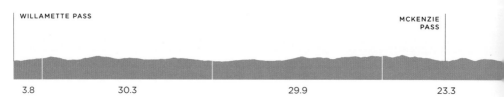

WILLAMETTE PASS

MCKENZIE PASS

3.8   30.3   29.9   23.3

Uytaahkoo

Karuk

—

Mount Shasta

M'laiksini Yaina

Klamath

—

Mount McLoughlin

Giiwas

Klamath

—

Crater Lake | Mount Mazama

14,179'

9,493'

6,178' (lake surface)
12,100' (before eruption)

The Skookum

Standing on the rim looking out over the lake, I saw a dust devil form about thirty feet in front of me. It came directly toward me, twirling over the ground. The wind blew across my face and I felt the spray of the spiraling sand and dirt. It circled around behind me as if it were some sort of malevolent spirit. The inanimate had become animate and I felt almost threatened by it, not wanting to let it out of my sight. It seemed to be sizing me up, determining my vulnerability. My skin stung from the sand as I watched it finally move on.

It Was the Best of Times, It Was the Worst of Times

And just like that, Crater Lake is gone and receding into the distance— thru-hikers have seen the last of its blue waters. Leave it to the PCT and its twisted sense of humor to follow that giant cauldron of water with some of the driest country thru-hikers have seen along the trail. Despite the lack of water, mosquitoes abound in late July when most northbound hikers pass through. A day that begins with arguably the most scenic highlight of the entire trail gives way to an utter lack of beauty—it is hot, dry, dusty, and miserable.

SANTIAM PASS

JEFFERSON PARK

22.7

27.3

35.2

Hisc'akwaleeas
Klamath

—

Mount Thielsen   Diamond Peak   Mount Bachelor

9,184'

8,540'

9,068'

Oregon Is Only Slightly Difficult

· Mosquitoes
· Dry stretches in Southern Oregon
· Mosquitoes
· Tree cover and lack of views
· Mosquitoes

TRAIL NOTES
Southbounders

I passed a southbound thru-hiker who assured me the mosquitoes would disappear in twenty miles or so. Whenever I met SoBo hikers I wanted to ask them a million questions. They were like omniscient beings, oracles really, who knew what my future held.

The Three Sisters

Mount Bachelor appears on the horizon. It is dark as a blackboard and the lingering patches of snow near its summit resemble white chalk markings. There are so few remaining that a hiker eating his lunch, if so inclined, could count them all—sixty-three in total. From there the PCT curves gracefully through a large meadow leading the eye directly toward the base of South Sister. Evergreens reach a quarter of the way up the mountain, followed by swirls of gray volcanic rock and white snowfields, and then finally the reddish crown of her summit. The trail follows along the volcano's base

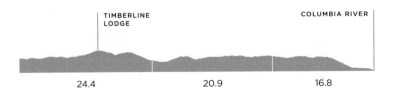

TIMBERLINE
LODGE

COLUMBIA RIVER

24.4   20.9   16.8

South Sister   Middle Sister   North Sister

10,363'   10,052'   10,090'

where a huge formation of rock and earth stands piled up like the ramparts of some castle, with South Sister the protected citadel. Creeks, cloudy with glacial till, flow over the trail one after the other, a welcome sight after so many stagnant lakes and ponds.

The Three Sisters Wilderness offers some of the most beautiful scenery since Crater Lake. It is a perfect subalpine mixture of meadows, streams, evergreens, and volcanic peaks. Each of the mountains possesses her own distinct look and personality. South Sister appears rounded and voluptuous. Middle Sister, with its symmetrically pyramidal shape, seems more poised and put together. North Sister is jagged and sharp, the most rebellious and wild of the trio.

The Skookum

As I neared Middle Sister the sky behind me grew dark with storm clouds. I felt as if I were being chased down,

hunted by something larger and more powerful than myself. I hiked furiously, hoping to stay ahead of it and bracing myself for the inevitable downpour. I felt completely vulnerable, as if I knew a gun were pointed at me and I was unable to do anything but wait, with no way to know when the trigger would finally be pulled. The sky blackened and threatened to engulf me. Thunder and lightning sounded from a distance, but I always seemed to be just on the edge of the storm, just out of reach. At one point I was convinced I could hear the sound of rain pelting the earth just behind me, yet I never felt a drop.

TRAIL NOTES

The Rest of Oregon

Oregon, as the thru-hiker discovers, is not only the land of tree cover and tiny lakes but also the land of fairy-tale, Matterhorn-like spires. From one viewpoint near McKenzie Pass, I could

Seekseekqua
Warm Springs
—

Mount Washington	Three Fingered Jack	Mount Jefferson

6,288'	7,844'	10,495'

see stretched out to the north a succession of volcanoes—Mount Washington, Three Fingered Jack, Mount Jefferson, and, surprisingly, Mount Hood, hazy and barely noticeable on the horizon. I could practically see the remainder of Oregon as it extends toward the Columbia River and its border with Washington.

TRAIL NOTES
The Ice Storm

As I drank beer in the town of Bend, the afternoon sky grew instantly dark and a hailstorm quickly materialized. Golf ball–sized chunks of ice slammed into the roof and the sides of the building, filling the open-air bar with a deafening clamor. Everyone got up and ran over to watch the spectacle, pulling out their phones to document the event. I remained where I was, the only person still seated. For everyone else it was a novelty, yet for me, knowing my time in town was nearly over and I would once again be out on the trail, the storm

evoked a much different response. All I could do was imagine what it would be like out on the PCT during such a storm. It was not a moment of wonder and excitement, but rather a strong reminder of just how vulnerable I was and how quickly the weather could change without warning. I sat there motionless, gripping my pint of beer tightly, staring out at the wall of people and the shower of ice beyond them.

Mount Jefferson Wilderness

On all sides, fires burn off in the distance. Smoke fills the air and the landscape appears almost post-apocalyptic—a gray and lifeless monochrome. In the distance, small lakes and ponds, each the color of ash, sit still and eerie among the skeleton forests that seem to extend unending toward the horizon. A mix of boulders and dead trees adorn the eroded hillsides and buzzards fly in tight circles overhead.

Mount Jefferson draws closer and closer. It disappears behind a ridge for

Wy'east	**Loowit**	**Pahto**
Multnomah	Klickitat	Klickitat
—	—	—
Mount Hood	Mount Saint Helens	Mount Adams

11,250'	8,366' (current)	12,280'
	9,677' (before eruption)	

several miles of the trail and then reappears, looming larger than one would ever have imagined. In the haze, the mountain and sky become nearly the same color, blending into one another. Jefferson seems to disappear, leaving its white snowfields to hover mysteriously in the air.

The Skookum

After turning a switchback I glanced down at my watch to check the temperature. The thermometer read 66.6 degrees. Only a few seconds later I pulled out my map and studied the route. I smiled at the uncanny coincidence of having just passed by a rock formation known as Devils Pulpit. As it turns out, toponyms named after the devil are fairly common in our nation's backcountry. *Devils Backbone. Devils Punchbowl. Devils Gulch*. I can count nearly twenty of them along the route of the PCT. For every Cathedral Rock one might pass along the trail, there are three

Devils Ridges. And it was in the wilderness after all that Satan is said to have tempted Jesus.

Wilderness was not always a thing of beauty or a place of recreation, but rather a place to be feared, full of danger and malevolence. As one early European settler put it several centuries ago, "Wilderness is a dark and dismal place where all manner of wild beasts dash about uncooked." Steinbeck observed in *Travels with Charley*, "how terrible the nights must have been in a time when men knew the things were there and were deadly." Later in the book he writes of the South Dakota Badlands, "They are like the work of an evil child. Such a place the Fallen Angels might have built as a spite to Heaven, dry and sharp, desolate and dangerous, and for me filled with foreboding. A sense comes from it that it does not like or welcome humans." All this ignores the fact that the so-called "wilderness" has long been inhabited and cared for by Indigenous peoples.

Tahoma	**Dakobed**	**Koma Kulshan**
Salish	Sauk-Suiattle	Lummi and Nooksack
—	—	—
Mount Rainier	Glacier Peak	Mount Baker

14,411'	10,541'	10,781'

TRAIL NOTES

Cascade Locks

[At the Cascade Locks Library] you can catch up on all the gruesome news you've been missing while out on the trail.

—*Pacific Crest Trail: Oregon & Washington* by Jeffrey P. Schaffer and Andy Selters (Wilderness Press, 1979 edition)

Current News (August 8, 2014) on CNN in Cascade Locks

· Tensions between Israel and Palestine have escalated
· Ebola outbreak in West Africa
· A new Islamic terrorist group named ISIS is gaining a hold in Iraq

In Iraq there were refugees hiding out atop a mountain ridge, hoping for food to be air dropped. The only way off the ridge was by mule trail, at the bottom of which stood men with guns waiting for anyone who came down. I was overwhelmed with guilt—irrational guilt perhaps—but guilt nonetheless. My day began as I hiked past a homeless man living in the woods outside of town, after which I rented a $100 cabin and stuffed my face with food. I was given free food. I was offered more free food by strangers. I wandered through idyllic natural landscapes while people around the world suffered. I walked in the mountains for pleasure while Iraqis hid atop ridges, certain death awaiting them should they descend. Yet when I descended from the mountains I found food, drink, lodging, and hospitality.

MOUNT
SHASTA

MOUNT
MCLOUGHLIN

CRATER
LAKE

DIAMOND
PEAK

MOUNT
BACHELOR

MOUNT
WASHINGTON

MOUNT
JEFFERSON

MOUNT
HOOD

MOUNT
SAINT HELENS

MOUNT
ADAMS

MOUNT
RAINIER

GLACIER
PEAK

Timberline Lodge and Mount Jefferson | Section G

The Bridge of the Gods (Klickitat Legend)

The two brothers Pahto and Wy'east both wished to settle along the Columbia River Gorge and quarreled over the land. To reconcile the dispute their father Sahale, chief of all the gods, shot out two arrows in opposite directions. Pahto followed the northbound arrow and settled there. Wy'east followed the southern arrow. Sahale then built Tamanawas, the Bridge of the Gods, over the Columbia to unite his family. The brothers soon fell in love with a beautiful woman named Loowit. They fought for her and in the ensuing battle villages and forests were destroyed. The Bridge of the Gods too was demolished and disappeared below the river, creating the Cascades of the Columbia. Sahale had no choice but to punish the three. Their fate was to forever stand motionless as a trio of volcanoes. Wy'east keeps his head lifted high in pride, forming a sharp peak known today as Mount Hood. Pahto keeps his head bent toward his beloved, forming the rounded summit known as Mount Adams. Loowit became the pre-eruption Mount Saint Helens, beautiful and perfectly symmetrical.

The Chinook Jargon

The Chinook Jargon was a nineteenth-century trade language used in the Pacific Northwest among American Indians and European traders and trappers. It originated in the lower Columbia River area and spread throughout Oregon and Washington and eventually on to British Columbia and Alaska. It was derived from the language of the Chinook peoples of the Columbia River, with the addition of French and English loan words. The language is sometimes referred to as the Chinuk Wawa (*wawa* means "speech" or "words"). The term *potluck*, as in "a potluck dinner," evolved from the Chinook Jargon word *potlatch*. The following are Chinook Jargon words used for toponyms on or near the Pacific Crest Trail.

Boston American
Boston Bluff, OR | Section C

Chikamin metal, ore
Chikamin Peak, WA | Section J

Chinook salmon
Chinook Pass, WA | Section I

Cultus worthless
Cultus Creek, WA | Section H

Hyak fast, hurry
Hyak Creek, WA | Section I

Hyas big, important
Hyas Lake, WA | Section J

Kaleetan arrow
Kaleetan Peak, WA | Section J

Lemolo wild, untamed
Lemolo Lake, OR | Section D

Lolo to carry
Lolo Pass, OR | Section G

Melakwa mosquito
Melakwa Lake, WA | Section J

Memaloose dead, to die
Memaloose Ridge, WA | Section K

Mesahchie evil, malign
Mesahchie Peak, WA | Section K

Moolack elk
Moolack Butte (near Elk Lake), OR | Section E

Mowich deer
Mowich Butte, WA | Section H

Olallie berry
Olallie Lake, OR | Section F

Siskiyou bob-tailed horse (may also be derived from the French *six cailloux*, meaning "six stones")
Siskiyou Peak, OR | Section B

Sitkum half, halfway, mixed-race
Sitkum Creek, WA | Section K

Skookum strong, powerful, monstrous
Skookum Meadow, WA | Section H

Tamanos spirit, power
Tamanos Mountain, WA | Section I

Tatoosh breasts
Tatoosh Range, WA | Section I

Tenas small, little, young
Tenas Peak, OR | Section D

Tyee chief, boss
Tyee Creek, OR | Section E

Mount Hood | Section G

TRAIL NOTES
A Low Point

As I situated myself within my shelter and got ready for bed my digital voice recorder was somehow switched on and I unknowingly recorded myself during a low point. These meltdowns inevitably occur when you are alone and feeling burnt out on the trail, but quickly fade from memory as they are overshadowed by far greater memories of beauty and grand adventure. I discovered the recording long after completing the trail and heard myself unfiltered. I felt as if I were intruding upon my past self as I listened to my own childish mutterings of discontent. Without any context it's hard to remember exactly what I was complaining about, aside from perhaps mosquitoes. It simply sounds like the expletive-laden ramblings of some lunatic. Was this what I sounded like every night as I prepared to fall asleep or during the day at the times I hiked alone along the trail?

Goddammit, this is so ridiculous.

Jesus.

Fuck man.

That's not good, whatever the hell that is [referring perhaps to a blister or cut on my foot].

[Loud flatulence]

Ugh, what a horrible smell.

I don't even know what the hell's going on there [referring to some other injury, rash, blister, or abrasion].

Is there another one in here [wondering if a mosquito made it into the tent]?

[Indecipherable muttering, followed by another moment of flatulence]

It's been a long time out here. Doing the same shit every day.

Is it really 9:30 already?

Ugh, itches so bad. When did that one happen? Must be a mosquito in here.

Goddamn man. Oh, these fucking mosquitoes. Ruining my life.

In Steinbeck's novella *The Red Pony*, the character Jody's grandfather recalls his emigration along the Oregon Trail and describes it as a great "westering."

THE JOURNEY

Oregon Trail	Pacific Crest Trail

THE DESTINATION

Willamette Valley	Canadian border

WHAT MATTERS

Not the destination, but rather the movement.
The slow steps that make the movement pile up until the continent is crossed.

A GROUP IS FORMED

The Beast	The Herd
Steinbeck describes them as a whole bunch of people made into one big crawling beast. Every man wanted something for himself, but the big beast that was all of them wanted only the movement.	The mass of thru-hikers slowly headed north along the PCT each summer could be aptly described as one big crawling beast—at least in Southern California. The Herd, as it is referred to by hikers, has yet to disperse across the landscape and thin out.

THE MOVEMENT IS STOPPED

The emigrants are eventually stopped by the Pacific. Steinbeck describes it as a line of men standing along the shore cursing the ocean because it stopped them. He writes that the westering has since died out of the people.	Thru-hikers travel up the rocky chain of the Pacific Crest. It is a great "northering" and it is not the ocean that stops them, but Canada. Instead of the coastline they find a giant clear-cut, a thin break in the great forest of the Pacific Northwest extending to both the east and west and marking with its erasure of the trees an international boundary and the end of a thru-hike.

Westering lives on in the long-distance hiker—whether it be westering, northering, southering, or eastering.

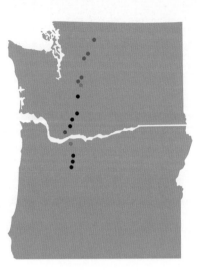

● Cascade blueberry

● Black huckleberry

● Thimbleberry

● Salmonberry

Berries

Most Delicious Berries of the Trail
Cutthroat Pass area, north of Highway 20 in Washington

The Latin Name for Cascade Blueberry is Very Accurate
Vaccinium deliciosum

Vintage Trail Blazes of the Pacific Crest Trail

In Oregon, thru-hikers begin to discover relics from the past—vintage, diamond-shaped PCT blazes nailed to the trees. Their design was adopted from the original Oregon Skyline Trail blazes, repurposed and modified for the newer and larger Pacific Crest Trail System. Some of these eighty-year-old enameled signs are rusted, others faded, and some simply monochromatic, their paint long since worn away. Some are covered in sap and some are barely visible, partially covered with bark and having been nearly swallowed by the tree itself.

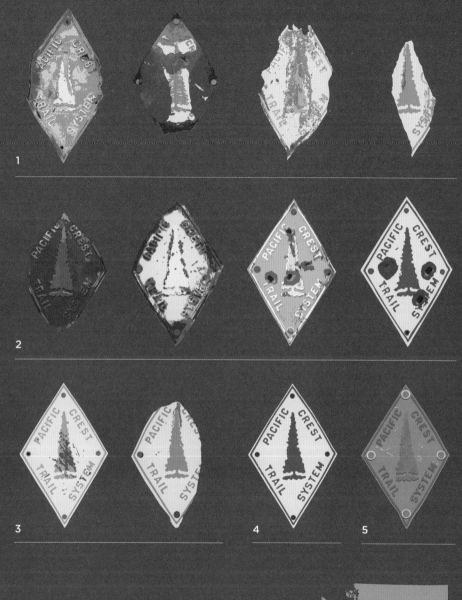

1

2

3   4   5

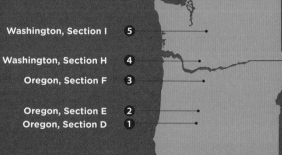

Washington, Section I   5
Washington, Section H   4
Oregon, Section F   3

Oregon, Section E   2
Oregon, Section D   1

Washington

THE NORTHERN CASCADES

There are times that one treasures for all one's life, and such times are burned clearly and sharply on the material of total recall.

JOHN STEINBECK
Travels with Charley

FAVORITE TOPONYMS

Bears Breast Mountain
Bullion Basin
Cutthroat Pass
Deadhead Lake
Deception Pass
Devils Stairway

Escondido Lake
Forlorn Lakes
Lake Valhalla
Laughingwater Creek
Little Ashes Lake
Lookingglass Lake
Madcat Meadow

Meander Meadow
Pickhandle Gap
Scimitar Glacier
Spark Plug Mountain
Spectacle Lake
Swimming Deer Lake
Three Fool's Creek

After the moderate terrain of Oregon, climbing up from sea level at the Columbia River Gorge can feel like a slap in the face. Southern Washington can be heavily forested, but eventually the PCT reaches the Indian Heaven Wilderness and its beautiful meadows and lakes. From there to the Canadian border, berries line the trail and tempt hikers to slow their pace. The Goat Rocks Wilderness is a highlight of the entire trail where, in good weather, Adams, Saint Helens, and Rainier are all visible as the hiker begins a dramatic traverse of the Knife's Edge, a high ridgeline walk that drops off precipitously on both sides. Northward the trail passes through the shadow of Washington's tallest peak and then enters the famed Alpine Lakes Wilderness and the subsequent Glacier Peak Wilderness, the most scenic and physically challenging section of the PCT since the High Sierra. It is the domain of the whistling marmot and the squeaking pika. Near the Suiattle River the PCT passes through a dark old-growth forest of massive Douglas firs and Western hemlock—the largest trees on the entire trail. From there, the hiker feels a sense of finality as they encounter the last trail town of Stehekin, the last road crossing and the last high pass of the trail. This final section passes through the wild and lonesome Pasayten Wilderness before ultimately reaching Monument 78 and the Canadian border.

REGION

5

MENTAL STRUGGLES

- Lack of motivation
- Burned out and tired of repetition
- Low morale due to rain
- Lonely
- Anxious about post-trail life

SONGS STUCK IN MY HEAD

Billy Joel, "Uptown Girl"
Diana Ross, "I'm Coming Out"
Linda Ronstadt and Aaron Neville, "Don't Know Much"
Sam Cooke, "What a Wonderful World"
Bruce Springsteen, "Glory Days"
Mike and the Mechanics, "All I Need Is a Miracle"
Nena, "99 Luftballons"
Twisted Sister, "We're Not Gonna Take It"
Cyndi Lauper, "Girls Just Want to Have Fun"
Daft Punk, "Get Lucky"
Christina Aguilera, "What a Girl Wants"
Miley Cyrus, "Wrecking Ball"
The Shins, "New Slang"
Michael Jackson, "Don't Stop 'til You Get Enough"
No Doubt, "Spiderwebs"
Starship, "Sara"
Ol' Dirty Bastard, "Shimmy Shimmy Ya"
Dire Straits, "Money for Nothing"
Bruce Springsteen, "Born in the USA"
Dr. Dre, "Nuthin' but a 'G' Thang"
Conan the Adventurer theme song
Oingo Boingo, "Weird Science"
Rockwell, "Somebody's Watching Me"

NOTES	MONTH	WEATH.	SECTION	MILE	DAY
	SEP	rain		2620.2	129
	moon	rain	L	2593.5	128
	moon	partly cloudy		2580.2	127
Banana slug seen	moon	sun		2553	126 🖼
	moon	sun			
Mount Rainier last seen at White Pass, Glacier Peak Wilderness	moon	sun		2500.3	124 🖼
First backcountry toilet (more common in WA)	moon	sun			
Baby frogs try to swim into water bottle at Pear Lake	moon	sun	K 🖼	2476	123
Three generations of hikers seen in a two-mile stretch: baby, parents, senior citizens	moon	sun		2445.6	121
Glacier Peak first seen	moon	rain		2420	120 🖼
Worst fall of the trail: fell onto right knee, took awhile to get back up	moon	partly cloudy	J	2380.6	117
Nights getting much colder	moon	partly cloudy			
Elk heard bugling					
Last dry stretch of the trail	moon	sun		2355.7	116
Last blister of the trail	moon	sun		2331.5	115
	moon	partly cloudy			
	moon	sun		2305.9	114 🖼
	moon	cloudy	I	2283.2	113
First and only mountain goat sighting	moon	rain		2264	112
Group of elk seen descending slope					
Trail completely washed out during worst rainstorm of the trail	moon	partly cloudy		2237.5	111
First bear grass sighting	moon	rain			
	moon	sun		2201.8	109
	moon	sun			
	moon	sun	H	2174.2	108

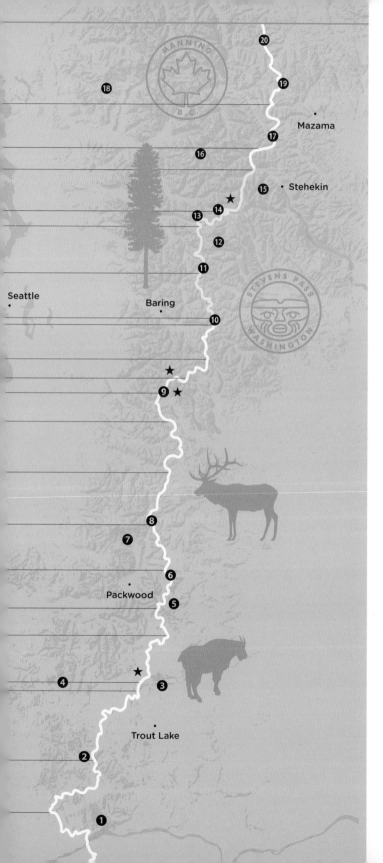

LANDMARKS

Junction with Pacific Northwest National Scenic Trail, 20

Harts Pass, last unpaved road, 19

Mount Baker, 18

Rainy Pass, last paved road, 17

North Cascades National Park, 16

Lake Chelan National Recreation Area, 15

Suiattle River and largest trees of the trail, 14

Fire Creek Pass and old Cascade Crest Trail sign, 13

Glacier Peak, 12

Cady Pass and 1920s tree carving, 11

Stevens Pass, 10

Snoqualmie Pass and old Cascade Crest Trail sign, 9

Chinook Pass, 8

Mount Rainier National Park, 7

White Pass and old Cascade Crest Trail sign, 6

Goat Rocks and old Cascade Crest Trail sign, 5

Mount Saint Helens, 4

Mount Adams, 3

Indian Race Track, 2

Columbia River, 1

Most scenic days or sections

★
Celebrity Sightings

Buddy Backpacker

Ron Strickland

Stringbean

Barely Missed Celebrity Sighting
Scott Williamson

Favorite part of the trail, best weather of the trail, and most solitude of the trail

Mount Adams as viewed from the Goat Rocks Wilderness | Section H

Washington Is a Joy to Hike
· Unless it rains a lot
· Oh, and there are 111,125 feet of elevation gain
· And 107,422 feet of elevation loss
· But otherwise it's over five hundred miles of glorious hiking
· Unless you get snowed on
· Oh, and the rodents

The Rodents

I was awoken by a thump at the edge of my sleeping pad, just above my head. I thought a twig must have fallen from the trees above and soon enough I fell back asleep. *Thump*. Even half asleep, I knew it was unlikely that something would fall twice in the same spot. I sat up and turned on my headlamp, scanning my surroundings. Nothing. A few minutes later, the same thing—a loud thump at the edge of my sleeping pad. Then again. And again. Finally, listening intently, I heard the sound of tiny paws scampering about the forest floor. Mice were running brazenly over the edge of my sleeping pad, throwing caution to the wind as they were lured by the food bag next to me. I inspected my food bag and found a tiny hole chewed into the side.

I HEARD THE scurrying of a mouse near my tent and, as a habit, reached out to shake the side of my shelter and scare it away. The rodent refused to flee and the sound of its little feet remained. Still half asleep it took me a moment to realize the mouse was *inside* my tent doing laps around me, tracing the edges of my tent

19.4   27.6   30.7   5

floor and occasionally running over my sleeping bag. When I unzipped the tent door, it calmly let itself out.

In the morning I retrieved my food bag from the nearby tree where I had hung it overnight, only to discover that mice had still gotten into it. It had been hanging by a thin cord from the upper limb of a tall tree, far from the trunk and a good five feet below the branch, yet somehow the mouse had made its way up the tree, across the branch, and down the cord to chew into my bag.

You Know You're a Thru-Hiker When . . .
A mouse gets into your food at night and the next morning you simply eat around the bite marks it left in your Pop-Tarts.

The Bridge of the Gods

A group of thru-hikers set foot upon the steel bridge and pass by its toll booth. There is no pathway for pedestrians, and the woman in the booth instructs them to simply walk against traffic. Ushered forth by 2,150 miles of memories, they cross over the mighty Columbia River on the Bridge of the Gods and walk triumphantly ahead toward Washington, cars slowing and moving aside to let them pass.

They cross the Columbia where once stood an earthen bridge, created long ago by violent landslides. The gods Wy'east and Klickitat had traveled that stone thoroughfare, but now they stand motionless and shielded in ice, keeping eternal vigilance on opposite sides of the river. In their minds, drunk on the pride of their achievements, the hikers ele-vate themselves to grandiose positions,

placing themselves among that pantheon of Cascadian gods. "We who walk across the Columbia are those who have walked every mile from southern lands," they think. "We who have walked from Mexico. We who spin the earth beneath us with each step, causing new peaks and ranges to rise on the horizon and familiar ones to recede off into the distance. *We thru-hikers! We gods among men!*"

Indian Race Track

Located less than a mile from the PCT, and reached by a side trail, is the Indian Race Track. Up until the early 1900s, during the summer berry season this area served as an annual gathering place for thousands of members of the Yakama, Klickitat, and Columbia River tribes, at a location along a historic cross-Cascades trade route. A track used for horse races, ten feet wide and over two thousand feet long, can still be seen in the large meadow.

The Chinook term for the area was Sahale Illahee, which means "Up Above Land" or "Heaven Land." The area is now known as the Indian Heaven Wilderness.

Ask a Thru-Hiker
Crossing over a Forest Service road I met a Yakama man and his daughter out picking berries.

"Are you finding any medicinal plants?" he asked me. "You doing any plant identification?"

"Well, all I'm really paying attention to right now are the berries," I answered.

He seemed to know almost nothing about the PCT.

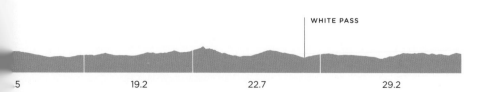

WHITE PASS

5   19.2   22.7   29.2

An equestrian and his horses make their way through the Glacier Peak Wilderness | Section K

"Why are you out here doing this?" he asked me.

I paused before answering and then gave my facetious response. "I like the pain and suffering."

"No, that's not pain and suffering," he said matter-of-factly, a rather serious look on his face. "I know why you're out here," he added mysteriously.

I waited for him to explain but he never did. He simply returned to his task of plucking berries.

TRAIL NOTES
Trout Lake

I continued on into the evening passing countless creeks and stopping often to gather handfuls of salmonberries. Occasionally Mount Adams revealed itself through a break in the trees. Vanilla leaf and inside-out flower carpeted the forest floor, their leaves growing in clusters of three. Something large crashed through the forest just out of sight. I scanned the greenery hoping to spot an elk but saw nothing and continued on.

The next morning I packed up as a light rain fell through the trees. I continued on to the Wind River Highway, where I turned right and began to walk toward the small town of Trout Lake. Mount Adams loomed ever closer just to the north. I caught up with another hiker and he called the hiker-friendly Trout Lake General Store to ask if we might get a ride. The woman on the other end called out to anyone in earshot, "Hey! Anybody want to go get some hikers?"

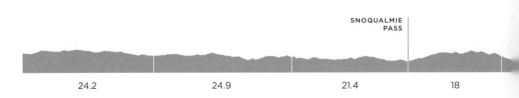

SNOQUALMIE
PASS

24.2   24.9   21.4   18

Someone volunteered and my companion proceeded to describe our appearance.

"I'm a tall guy with a beard and a green shirt. My buddy has a hat and a blue shirt . . ."

The woman cut him off. "Yeah, you'll be the only people walking down the road."

At the store we rented a room for a song and then made our way to the Bear Creek Café, often the only restaurant in town that is open. The café is connected to a service station, and the whole operation seems to be run by the same family.

The afternoon temperature began to rise and four of us hikers made our way down to Trout Lake Creek. Rusty metal pilings rose up out of the water,

remnants of some long-ago dismantled bridge. The water was ice cold and we stepped gingerly over jagged rocks on the creek bed, making our way out to the deepest point. As we swam, we nervously eyed the sky to the north. Thunderstorms were rolling in. The sky grew dark and rain began to fall off in the distance.

We made our way back to the store just as a heavy rain began to fall upon Trout Lake. We crammed into a tiny room above the store. Three of us were able to claim our own beds, while the shortest in our group opted to sleep in the closet. With four thru-hikers packed into the small room it grew hot and, as one might expect, began to smell. We drank beer and ate ice cream. We

STEVENS
PASS

25.6   22.9   7.5   24.3   26.7

ALDER VANILLA LEAF BROADLEAF LUPINE WHITE INSIDE-OUT FLOWER

watched videos on a smartphone of Robin Williams stand-up routines. The comedian and actor had taken his own life the day before. To amplify the sound, we placed the phone in a metal cooking pot and then all lay there, listening and laughing together.

TRAIL NOTES
Goat Rocks Wilderness

The rain grew heavier and heavier as I traveled through the Goat Rocks. Though I felt strong and resilient as a thru-hiker, with the endless succession of sunny days I was in many ways no better-equipped to deal with bad weather than I had been before my thru-hike. After 2,200 miles I was really only experiencing for the first time what it was like to set up camp in heavy rain, with all of my gear quickly becoming damp. I hadn't experienced any heavy rain since the night before Mammoth Lakes, when I still had much of California ahead of me. In Oregon, afternoon thunderstorms had chased me down but never quite followed through on their threats.

The Knife's Edge

Mount Adams finally reveals itself in the early morning light, its summit dusted in fresh snow. Parts of the valley below are visible amidst patches of swirling fog. The trail heads north through meadows of wildflowers that dot the landscape in red, white, and blue. Bear grass floats buoyantly, its white clusters of flowers ballooning out of tall stalks that sway in the breeze. The PCT climbs higher into a landscape of rock and snow and ice, while to the south, Adams is slowly enveloped by fog and clouds, leaving only a featureless backdrop of sullen gray.

The trail approaches the Knife's Edge, where it continues along the spine of a long, sheer ridgeline that drops dramatically on either side into forested valleys far below. One by one a succession of thru-hikers begins the precarious traverse, appearing as silhouettes against the white nothingness. Snowfields on either side stretch down and merge with the foggy white of everything beyond the ridge. Mount Rainier is out there somewhere behind all the white. There is a roller coaster of ups and downs along

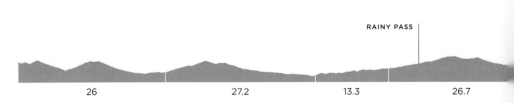

RAINY PASS

26 27.2 13.3 26.7

BUNCHBERRY   VINE MAPLE   THREELEAF   DEVIL'S CLUB
                                        FOAMFLOWER

that rocky spine until the trail drops into a wet and verdant landscape. An old wooden Cascade Crest Trail sign lay shattered among the rocks.

Ask a Thru-Hiker

I reached Sheep Lake where colorful tents dotted the many campsites, their occupants only beginning to stir on that lazy Sunday morning. A little girl approached and I expected her to shyly pass by, but instead she called out to me, "Hi! How are you?"

"Good! How are you?" I replied.

"It's just the prettiest, isn't it?" she asked precociously. She then shouted to her father, back at their nearby campsite, "Can I hike a little further to the viewpoint?"

"Breakfast is going to be ready in a minute if you want to get it while it's hot," he called back to her.

She paused for a moment, considering her options, then sprinted past me back toward her campsite, food having won out over the scenery. I could hardly blame her.

A LOCAL BACKPACKER unleashed a barrage of questions. He had a horrible case of the hiccups, which became interspersed throughout his interrogation, making it all the more intolerable.

"What? You don't [hiccup] wear leather boots? You wear running shoes?

"How many [hiccup] miles are you hiking each day?

"You don't have a tent? Just a tarp? What? You use your [hiccup] trekking poles to stand up your tarp? What are you [hiccup] doing? Hanging between them like a *frickin'* hammock?"

He wandered over and started picking up and examining another hiker's drying gear.

"You really shouldn't go to Stevens Pass!" he lectured us. "You should [hiccup] go out the Surprise Lake Trail—it's so much [hiccup] closer to Skykomish!"

"Yeah, but then we wouldn't be hiking the PCT," I said.

"Well, in that case, you should go up and over [hiccup] Surprise Mountain, not around it! That used to be the actual PCT route!"

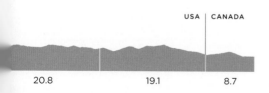

USA | CANADA

20.8   19.1   8.7

SHINY CINNAMON
POLYPORE
& INDIAN
STRAWBERRY

FLY AGARIC

BROWN FUNNEL
POLYPORE

PLUMS &
CUSTARD

TRAIL NOTES
Hiker Haven

Along with the Saufleys and the Andersons, Jerry and Andrea Dinsmore were the third in a triumvirate of iconic PCT trail angels. In 2003, Jerry Dinsmore invited three thru-hikers back to his home, thinking they were homeless and in need of help. He soon learned they were hiking the PCT, and Hiker Haven was born. They hosted hikers each year since and became particularly adept at helping northbound hikers make wise decisions regarding the potentially dangerous weather north of Stevens Pass.

When I visited in 2014 plastic pink flamingos adorned the yard. Andrea's license plate read PCT MOM, and next to it was a bumper sticker that stated *Hug a logger. You'll never go back to trees.* Hikers did their laundry and wandered about in borrowed clothing. One woman wore a tiny dress, revealing a smattering of tattoos. A male hiker donned a dress as well, the hair on his shoulders and back sticking out in large patches. A German hiker joked in his thick accent, "You look silly . . . *but sexy.*"

Jerry Dinsmore, clad in suspenders and a vintage Kenworth trucks shirt, pulled up a chair alongside me and we sat and watched as a train rolled past loaded down with airplanes en route to the Boeing facility near Seattle. They were only fuselages, devoid of their wings.

"There's a tunnel a few miles back with a pile of wings next to the entrance," he joked.

Another thru-hiker, fresh from Stevens Pass, was dropped off in the driveway. Andrea greeted him, reaching out her arm to shake hands. He instinctively stuck out his closed hand, offering the customary thru-hiker fist bump.

"Oh, that's not gonna go over well," Jerry said, laughing.

THE PCT COMMUNITY lost a very special member with the passing of Andrea in 2017. Jerry still welcomes hikers to his home in Baring.

Rest in Peace
Andrea Kay Burr-Dinsmore
"PCT Mom"
1949–2017

Glacier Peak Wilderness

The surrounding ridges are carpeted in luminous green meadows lit up by the morning sun. The sky is free of haze and the surrounding mountains are crystal clear as far as the eye can see. Rainier

| CANDY CAP | ROSY SLIME SPIKE | BLOODY BRITTLEGILL | HEMLOCK VARNISH SHELF |

still reveals itself from time to time, peeking over southern ridges. Marmots whistle from the berry bushes, their heads protruding up from the leaves like periscopes as they scan their surroundings. The trail at times crosses over snowfields and then past small Mica Lake, which still harbors floating ice. With September drawing near the ice is unlikely to melt before the snow once again begins to fall—it has been victorious in its resistance to summer.

Glacier Peak seems to be Washington's forgotten volcano—due in part to its location within a large, roadless wilderness area. From surrounding areas there are fewer dramatic views of the mountain than there are of Adams, Rainier, or Baker. It tends to blend in with the tall, jagged peaks surrounding it. The thru-hiker, however, gets to know the volcano intimately as the PCT skirts along its base and crosses the creeks draining its slopes, gaining and losing thousands of feet of elevation in the process.

Stehekin

From Suiattle Pass the landscape seems to gradually tilt downward toward the horizon, and hikers can look forward to a descent all the way to Stehekin, the final trail town of the PCT—famous in thru-hiker lore for its bakery. It sits secluded at the northern tip of Lake Chelan, accessible only by boat, plane, or hiking trail. To say that it's remote is an understatement. The PCT brings hikers to the end of the single road that leads into town. From there they can get on the National Park Service shuttle or perhaps catch a ride with a local fisherman. Stehekin is small and compact, with an idyllic location amidst the lake and mountains. All the vehicles parked at the ferry landing seem at least four or five decades old, only adding to the feeling that time stands still in this lakeside town. Hikers can set up for the night in a tiny campground perched on a miniature bluff above the water, watching brightly colored float planes land upon the lake's surface and skim to a halt. When night falls, the view of the Milky Way is breathtaking. Stehekin translates to "the way through," an appropriate name for a trail town on a thru-hike.

STEHEKIN'S MAIN ROAD curves around the marshy northernmost tip of Lake Chelan where the Little Boulder Creek empties into the lake. It is the extreme end of a fifty-mile body of water that narrowly snakes through the mountains down to the dry and sunbaked wine

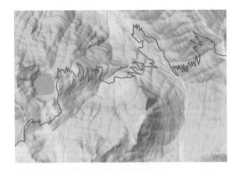

The Serpentine Switchbacks of Section K

Climbing up from Milk Creek, hikers encounter around eighty-one switchbacks in just eight miles, perhaps the highest concentration of switchbacks on the trail.

country of Central Washington, so drastically different from the often overcast and rainy North Cascades. An old Chevy pickup truck passes by on the road. Owned by the Stehekin Pastry Company, it is on its way down to the boat landing. A girl and dog sit atop the wooden flatbed of the truck. Further down the road is a beautiful garden full of cabbage, kale, and other produce. A row of dahlias line a pathway, the intricately geometrical puffs of each flower leading the way toward an apiary buzzing with honey bees. On a bench rests a pile of rainbow chard, the leaves bright green and glossy and the stems neatly arranged in shifting hues of orange, yellow, and purple. The bakery truck passes again, headed back in the other direction. This time the girl sits in the passenger seat and the flatbed is piled high with boxes and goods that have been boated in. The little dog is positioned atop the huge pile with his chest puffed out, standing guard over his precious cargo.

Racist Toponym along the PCT That Has Been Changed

Coon Lake > Howard Lake

Wilson Howard was an African American prospector who lived by the lake in the late nineteenth century. He was one of only two black miners at that time working in the North Cascades. Washington State changed the name in 2007. It took eight years for the federal government to adopt the changes in maps, trail signs, and tourist information.

Glacier Pass

A hiker climbs the trail up to Glacier Pass shrouded in a complete whiteout. From time to time, however, a small break appears in the mist and a window opens on an abstract pattern composed of brown rock and white snowfields. Then, as quickly as it had appeared, it vanishes. With time, however, the clouds begin to burn off and more windows soon form. The breaks in the clouds remain open and they grow. It begins to feel as if one were putting together a giant jigsaw puzzle, each opening in the clouds revealing a new piece. Slowly, more sections of the puzzle are added, and a mountain scene forms. Then, as the hiker nears the pass, the clouds and fog come rolling back in and obliterate the image, like someone tilting a table and sending the puzzle pieces crashing to the floor.

The Pasayten

On the other side of Cutthroat Pass a whole new array of peaks reveal themselves. They seem to scrape the dark, low-hanging clouds. The mountains are drier, more barren, and the color of sand—tans and beiges and browns. Tall, slanted peaks all seem to angle up in the same direction, and the trail curves along slopes high above a perfectly

Ephemera and imagery found in the trail town of Stehekin

rounded valley scoured long ago by glaciers. The valley extends off into the distance looking like the gutter to some massive bowling lane.

The PCT enters a thin forest of larch. In a month's time their needles will change color and they will light up in a brilliant gold. Lucky are those hikers who arrive to the Pasayten late in the season and see the colors at their most brilliant. It is a wilderness so different from the western crest of the Cascades. It looks more arid, the trees grow more sparsely, and a golden-green grass covers the slopes. It feels lonelier and more remote. The cloud cover hangs low but not so low that it obscures the sea of peaks in every direction.

The trail pushes on, deeper into the wild and lonesome Pasayten. A cold wind rustles the grass of a small meadow and it sways from side to side. Off to the east, shafts of sunlight break through the clouds and light up small spots on the valley floor. Hovering above the surrounding peaks is a little, defiant patch of blue sky. A calm pervades the scene. To the north the trail passes through the meadow and disappears into the trees. It is the one constant view along the thru-hiker's journey—the trail heading ever northward. Through desert, snowy peaks, volcanoes, valleys, canyons, and sweltering tree cover. Past saplings and seven hundred-year-old firs. Past lakes and waterfalls and boiling mud pots. Past tiny mountain streams and rivers as mighty as the Columbia. Soon enough, though, the trail will come to an end. The wind picks up again and raindrops begin to strike the blades of grass.

Washington's Old-Growth Giants

The trail climbs to a ridgeline with views in every direction. A massive, pyramid-shaped butte rises from a valley like the back of some prehistoric creature emerging from the primordial forests below. The PCT then drops for what seems like an eternity down to the Suiattle River and enters a magical section of old-growth forest. As John Vaillant writes in his book *The Golden Spruce*, "The atmosphere in an old-growth coastal rainforest borders on the amniotic; still and close, sound moves differently in here, and the air moves hardly at all." In *Travels with Charley*, Steinbeck wrote similarly of the giant redwoods of his native Northern California: "There's a cathedral hush here. Perhaps the thick soft bark absorbs sound and creates a silence."

Hikers slow as they pass through, their heads swiveling in all directions, entranced by the sheer girth and height of those trees. It is almost disorienting, and with the silence, stillness and heaviness of the air, it feels more like one is hiking along the ocean floor rather than through a forest. It isn't hard to imagine these trees as sentient beings, aware of one's presence in the forest. Steinbeck felt the same: "To me there's a remote and cloistered feeling here. One holds back speech for fear of disturbing something—what? From my earliest childhood I've felt that something was going on in the groves, something of which I was not a part. . . . These huge things that control the day and inhabit the night are living things and have presence, and perhaps feeling, and, somewhere in deep-down perception, perhaps communication."

As it turns out, Steinbeck was right. Trees do in fact possess a means of communication, though not of course speech as we know it. Fungi help to form subterranean communication networks that connect the root systems of the old-growth trees. Through these networks, mother trees can recognize their offspring and adjust their competitive behaviors accordingly. When one tree becomes shaded from the sun and its ability to photosynthesize thus hindered, another can funnel sugars to it. When a tree is attacked by pests, it can in turn send out chemical signals to warn its neighbors, so that they may hastily produce defensive enzymes.

The Final Night

I arrived at a large and empty campsite and went about the business of pitching my tarp. At one point I glanced up to see a deer watching me. I continued with my chores, pulling out my nearly empty food bag and realizing it was the last time I would feel the joy of knowing a town was near—soon civilization would be *all* I knew.

I watched a chipmunk run around the campsite and then zip up a forty-foot-tall snag and disappear into a hole at the very top. *The energy you must expend*, I thought. *You must be constantly eating. I suppose you're not too different from a thru-hiker*. More deer arrived, foraging in the grass as they moved around my shelter. As the light faded and the forest grew black, the deer became dark shapes slowly circling. It was eerie, but at the same time comforting, as if they were guardians. One was only a few feet away and I could hear it chewing as I lay down to sleep. They remained long after night fell, and I woke from time to time as they grazed. In the morning, they were gone.

The Skookum

I ate lunch looking down on Hopkins Lake, a bluish-gray circle sitting in a little basin far below. A flock of birds appeared below me as they flew over the lake, their dark shapes standing out in contrast to the lighter color of the water. They continued on over the forest and then vanished. Blending in with the trees, their movement became imperceptible. It was as if the lake had been a window open to a different place, where the birds existed in another world apart from my own.

THE TRAIL BOTTOMED out in dark tree cover and a loud noise broke the silence. In that lonely eeriness of the forest it sounded almost like a witch cackling. Out of the corner of my eye I saw movement. Something shot by me in a blur, headed in the opposite direction. It looped back around and flew by me again, and I realized it was a pileated woodpecker, the red plumage of its head clearly visible. I stood on a slope, slightly above the bird as it soared by through the trees, its wings outspread. I was amazed at the breadth of its wingspan, so much larger than I would have imagined.

The Border

I looked out over the trail as it twisted and turned down into a basin before making its final large climb up to Woody Pass. It was exciting, staring out at the final pass of the entire PCT. A small bit of snow sat in the notch between two rounded peaks. I froze in the biting wind as I descended, then began to sweat as I made the climb up to the pass. Hawks filled the sky above the trail as it cut across long slopes beneath high ridges. My titanium cooking pot hung from the outside of my pack and made a clanging noise that sounded much like a cowbell. I felt instantly transported back to Northern California, where so many cows had grazed alongside the trail. Sound and smell can evoke such strong memories, and for an instant there on my final day I shot back a thousand miles to the mountains above Etna.

There was a great sense of peace during those last few days on the trail, in that womblike atmosphere of an overcast Pacific Northwest day, stuck in the liminal zone between earth and the

What's in a Name?

Albert H. Sylvester is credited with naming over one thousand natural features in Washington's Cascade Range. As national forests proliferated, it became necessary to create detailed maps and place names, particularly in the interest of fighting forest fires. In the early twentieth century, many places in the Cascades had not yet been explored by white settlers. Therefore, in the first part of the twentieth century, Sylvester found himself in both the adventurous and creative role of exploring and naming the backcountry, given carte blanche in his creation of toponyms. He adopted several standard conventions in his naming.

Toponyms in bold lie directly on or adjacent to the PCT.

PATTERNED NAMING
· Aurora Creek and Borealis Ridge
· Choral Creek and Anthem Creek
· Royal Creek, Crescent Creek, and Schilling Creek (named after popular baking powder brands at the time)
· **Bryant Peak, Irving Peak, Whittier Peak, Longfellow Mountain,** and **Poe Mountain** (named for American poets)
· **Indian Pass** and Indian Creek were named for the ancient American Indian trail over the pass, along with nearby Indian Head Peak and Papoose Creek.
· Kloochman Creek and Tillicum Creek (Chinook Jargon terms for "wife" and "friend")
· **Labyrinth Mountain** (inspired by its dense network of topographical contour lines on a map) and nearby Minotaur Lake and Theseus Lake.

WHIMSICAL NAMING
· **Overcoat Peak** (Sylvester left his coat buttoned around a surveying cairn on the peak)
· Dirtyface Peak (named for its dirt-stained snowbanks during the spring melt)
· **Dishpan Gap** (named for a rusty dishpan found at this terminus of a popular sheepherding trail)
· Fifth of July Mountain (simply the day Sylvester was there, a wink at the overabundance of Fourth of July toponyms in the region)
· **Kodak Peak** (his assistant lost a Kodak camera here)
· **Pass-no-Pass** (a pass devoid of road or trail, only suitable for sheepherders in Sylvester's opinion)
· Candy Creek (named for its sweet taste)
· Grindstone Creek (named for a grindstone that had fallen from a pack horse as it forded the creek)
· Tinpan Mountain (named for no other reason than "it was just a name for a place needing naming")
· Frosty Meadow (named when Sylvester woke in the morning to find his camp covered in rime and hoarfrost)
· **Lake Janus** (named after the two-faced Roman god, because Sylvester discovered that the lake, depicted in older maps as draining to the west, in fact drained to the east)

SPECIFIC PEOPLE
· Cool Creek (named not for its refreshing nature but for a prospector named Thomas Cool)
· Klone Peak (named not for a person, but for Sylvester's dog)

- Crook Mountain (originally known as Goat Mountain but renamed for an Army officer because according to Sylvester there were already more Goat Mountains than actual goats in the Northwest)

NAMING LAKES FOR WOMEN
- **Josephine Lake** (named for the wife of a forest ranger)
- **Lake Sally Ann** (not named for an actual woman; rather, Sylvester conjured the name because it seemed to "fit like a hand in a glove")

Sylvester believed the most beautiful area in the Cascades was the area around Buck Creek Pass, reached from the PCT via a side trail on the long climb up to Suiattle Pass in Washington's Section K.

East of where the PCT would eventually travel, at the age of seventy-three, Sylvester was mortally wounded near two lakes he had named, the result of his horse panicking and falling down a steep and rocky slope. Nearby Sylvester Lake was named in his honor.

Reckoning With the Past

It is important to acknowledge that many of the places in the mountains of California, Oregon, and Washington were already named by indigenous peoples, long before anyone of European descent "discovered" them. There are many stories to tell about the land the Pacific Crest Trail travels through and it would take many books to tell them all.

Here Are Two Places to Start:
Dispossessing the Wilderness: Indian Removal and the Making of the National Parks, Mark David Spence

As Long as Grass Grows: The Indigenous Fight for Environmental Justice from Colonization to Standing Rock, Dina Gilio-Whitaker

It is an unfortunate fact that many of the names encountered during a thru-hike of the PCT, and in this book as a result, belong to men who espoused racist views. Gifford Pinchot was a delegate to the International Eugenics Congress. Joseph LeConte, a member of the Sierra Club for whom several places in the High Sierra are named, was a critic of Reconstruction and the enfranchisement of African Americans. John Muir, so concerned with the plight of wildlife and the natural world, failed to extend this affection toward his fellow members of the human race. He recalled the supposed laziness of African Americans during his long walk from the Midwest to the South. He spoke of the "dirty and irregular" life of the Ahwahnechee living in the Merced River Valley. He assured prospective white visitors to national parks that most American Indians "are dead or civilized into useless innocence." National parks like Yosemite and Yellowstone are world-renowned for their preservation of this country's most beautiful natural landscapes. While visions of pristine, uninhabited nature led to the creation of these parks, they also inspired policies of Indian removal, ignoring the fact that these preserves had been inhabited for thousands of years.

Some Native Lands Traveled
on the Pacific Crest Trail

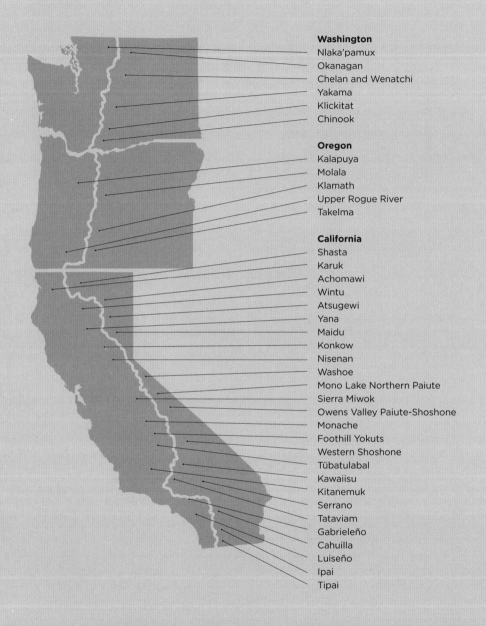

Washington
Nlaka'pamux
Okanagan
Chelan and Wenatchi
Yakama
Klickitat
Chinook

Oregon
Kalapuya
Molala
Klamath
Upper Rogue River
Takelma

California
Shasta
Karuk
Achomawi
Wintu
Atsugewi
Yana
Maidu
Konkow
Nisenan
Washoe
Mono Lake Northern Paiute
Sierra Miwok
Owens Valley Paiute-Shoshone
Monache
Foothill Yokuts
Western Shoshone
Tübatulabal
Kawaiisu
Kitanemuk
Serrano
Tataviam
Gabrieleño
Cahuilla
Luiseño
Ipai
Tipai

low-hanging clouds above. I enjoyed the solitude and clarity of my final days on the trail. My mind and body felt as crisp and sharp as the oncoming fall. I was coming to the end of something, an irresistible momentum carrying me forward to the completion of the trail, and I had no idea what would happen afterward, no idea what lay on the other side. I reached Castle Pass and then entered forest, much of it interspersed with snags and fallen trees. There were some views, but I hiked mostly in tree cover. I pulled out my map wondering where I was and realized I had only three-tenths of a mile to go. I was only moments from finishing.

I arrived at the wooden structure that marks the northern terminus of the Pacific Crest Trail, nearly identical to the one that had greeted me at Campo. Monument 78—a small metal obelisk—marks the international border and commemorates the Treaty of 1846, which set the boundary of the United States and Canada at the forty-ninth parallel. At Campo the border had been marked by a metal fence; here in the Pacific Northwest it is denoted by a clear cut in the forest, only a dozen or so feet wide and extending off to the east and west. There was no one else there. I cracked open a beer I had been carrying, picked up from some trail magic at Harts Pass, and sat in the dirt next to my pack as I had done countless times before. Above me the clouds disappeared and the sun shined down upon that little clearing in the forest I and so many other thru-hikers had devoted our summer to reaching.

PLASTIC HAWAIIAN LEIS encircled the bottom of Monument 78 and I noticed it sat slightly off-kilter atop its base. I removed it to reveal a trail register and other notes and mementos left by past hikers. I rummaged through them and pulled out a small plastic bag that seemed to be filled with sand. A note inside read:

Kevin Huthman, 1981–2009
Section hiked 2,200 miles of the PCT
before dying of lupus in 2009
His spirit completed the trail today,
8/19/2014

He was born the same year I was and had not lived to see his thirtieth birthday. He never saw the wooden terminus, that metal obelisk or the clear-cut in the trees. He never wandered through the lonely Pasayten and counted down the miles to the end of his final section hike of the PCT. I knew only two things about him: we would have been the same age were he still alive and we had hiked 2,200 of the same miles along the trail, Kevin ticking off sections over many summers and me doing it as a thru-hike in the same year that his family carried that plastic bag in their packs and finally placed it within Monument 78. Presumably, it contained some of his ashes.

Some months after completing the PCT I did an online search for Kevin Huthman and clicked on his obituary. There was a small black-and-white photo of a smiling young man. He was unshaven and wore glasses. He looked like any young man I may have met on the trail that year. He had been valedictorian of his graduating class, earned a degree in computer science, and gotten engaged. In the end, he had succumbed to multiple organ failures.

I found his father's hiking website and photo albums organized by each section of the PCT. The photos show Kevin and his family hiking various sections of the PCT over the course of many summers, as far back as 1990. Clearly I did not know him, but looking at a photo of him as a child smiling at the camera I felt overwhelmed with emotion. He had no idea he would die so young. His parents did not know, nor his brother, nor his sister. I clicked through the photos, recognizing shots almost identical to ones I had taken, little having changed in the years separating them. I saw a young Kevin posing in shorts and short sleeves, standing on skinny legs that hardly seemed like they could propel him up and over the high passes of the Sierras. I saw him perched atop the southern terminus monument. I saw him peeking out from below a Joshua tree. He hiked down the trail with his brothers, carrying external frame packs nearly as big as they were. He stood at Forester Pass in 1994 high above the spot where I had camped. There was a photo of him a decade later, just north of the California/Oregon border, atop a large rock formation, lying on his stomach with arms and legs outstretched like Superman as he hovered thirty feet over his campsite below. I saw him in Oregon, caught in mid-step as he wandered through a mass of butterflies congregating at the shore of a pond, many of them captured in flight as they fluttered around his body and head. I saw him posing at Sister Mirror Lake, his arm around his younger sister. And I saw photos of his sister and father continuing their section hike of the PCT after Kevin's death, until they finally completed the trail in the same summer I had.

SOON OTHER HIKERS began to arrive, and within half an hour there were six of us at the border. I sat back and watched the show, as hikers acted out carefully choreographed scenarios they had long planned. One hiker made a raucous entrance, dancing and singing as he embraced the terminus. He changed

into American flag shorts, slipped on a shirt with a huge bald eagle graphic and donned an oversized straw hat. He set up his camera to record, then pulled out his speakers and began to play music. Next he produced a bottle of Canadian Club Whisky he had carried from Stehekin and climbed atop the wooden structure to recite a well-rehearsed speech to the accompaniment of Sister Sledge's "He's the Greatest Dancer." Two hikers from Germany unfurled their country's flag and posed for photos atop the terminus monument. A Dutch thru-hiker did the same. Everyone passed around the Canadian Club and took swigs from the bottle. I sat back and soaked it all in, happy for the quiet time of reflection I had experienced and also glad to witness the other side of the coin—the exuberant revelry of a thru-hike completed. Eventually I stood up and made my way across the border into Canada. As I stepped across that imaginary line a perfectly timed gust of cold wind blew through the trees and hit me, as if to punctuate both my thru-hike and the summer season in the mountains.

Epilogue

AS YOU HIKE mile after mile across three states you imagine that final moment of reaching the border to be an overwhelming experience, assuming the gravity of it will hit you like a ton of bricks. In reality, however, when you've lived out every month and week and day and hour and minute and second that transpires between Mexico and Canada, it's not quite as dramatic as you might expect. There was no surprise in the end, but the sense of accomplishment was hardly diminished. And with it came the realization that it was all over and I was headed back to real life, full of its own unique joys and difficulties. I couldn't stay on the trail forever, nor did I wish to. I simply hoped to find the next big thing to work toward, the next passion that would consume me from waking until bedtime.

While the PCT had officially ended, I still had over eight miles of trail leading me to Manning Provincial Park and its lodge. The morning felt dark and dreary and it was easy to believe summer was finished. Fall was quickly approaching, with the dark and wet Pacific Northwest winter fast on its heels. I reached the end of the trail as it met a paved road and that was that. After 2,659 miles and over four months of walking, the trail simply ended. There was nothing else to do but dump the rocks from my shoes and begin the short road walk to the lodge. I rounded the last corner and came to an abrupt stop as a Greyhound bus pulled out in front of me. I looked up at its tinted windows, wondering if anyone I knew was inside. I squinted, focusing my eyes, and I could just make out the shapes of people behind the glass. They began to wave their arms at me and bang on the windows, yet the tinted glass continued to obscure their identities. It was a large group of hikers that had remained only a day ahead of me ever since Snoqualmie Pass. I had finally caught up to them. On that bus were hikers I had gotten to know over the course of hundreds and hundreds of miles. I was sad not to be able to see their faces, but raised my arms up in the air triumphantly, grinning from ear to ear and tickled by the timing of it all. The bus turned the corner, pulled out onto Highway 3, and continued on toward Vancouver.

IN THE FINAL PAGES of Steinbeck's novel *Tortilla Flat*, the protagonist falls into a deep depression and death draws near to him. He had lost the freedom he once knew and that change in his life led to a dark, downward spiral. One of his friends recalls seeing him in his final days. "I looked at him, and then I saw something else. At first it looked like a black cloud in the air over Danny's head. And then I saw it was a big black bird, as big as a man. It hung in the air like a hawk over a rabbit hole. I crossed myself and said two Hail Marys."

That same omen of a black bird was hovering above me as well. It had been following me north along the entire length of the trail, but I had hiked fast enough to avoid it. With my journey finished at Highway 3 in Canada I looked up to see it above me, emblazoned on a road sign, its eyes void and empty and a piercing white. It was the emblem of the Crowsnest Highway, named for Crowsnest Pass further east along the Continental Divide where a list of tragedies had occurred. Over the span of five decades an explosion at a mine killed 128 men, a landslide buried one town and killed 90 of its residents, and a forest fire destroyed another. In a second mining disaster, Canada's worst, the lives of 189 men were snuffed out. Thirty years later an airplane disappeared into the side of a mountain along with everyone on board.

REGARDING HIS TIME living in the Sierra Nevada, Steinbeck wrote in a letter to a friend, "You see, dear, the mountains did things to me. The long hermitage put an uncontrollable irritability very near the surface. I am pettish and small, and sullen. The mountains are not supposed to do this but they did."

The mountains, as it turned out, had done things to me as well—things they were not supposed to do. Transitioning back into life after the trail was as hard as I imagined it would be and then some. I sank into a depression unlike anything I had ever experienced. It lasted nearly five months and it took me longer to pull myself up out of that dark hole than it did to walk across all of California, Oregon, and Washington. I went from the experience of living life to its fullest to barely wanting to live at all.

STEINBECK MENTIONS IN *The Log from the Sea of Cortez* that with human beings, "coordination and disintegration follow each other with great regularity." He writes that there is no "lostness" like that which a man experiences when

a perfect pattern has dissolved about him. There is no hater like one who has greatly loved. For the thru-hiker, the trail is that perfect pattern and that great love. Post-trail depression is the ensuing disintegration.

This depression is a fairly common experience for many thru-hikers. Thru-hiking is an activity that requires extreme amounts of exertion and in turn yields extreme amounts of exhilaration for months on end. Over that time, the thru-hiker becomes desensitized to the endorphins, dopamine, adrenaline, and other chemicals the body releases. Once the trail is over, one is so desensitized that the normal levels of activity in day-to-day life fail to create even a moderate sense of well-being, let alone the sheer exhilaration of a thru-hike. That shift in the brain's chemistry, coupled with the often challenging experience of assimilating back into "normal life," can lead to post-trail blues that can spiral out of control into the clinical depression I experienced.

Nature has been shown to have a significant positive effect on one's mental health. Thru-hikers become accustomed to these effects and spend their days living mostly in the moment. The harsh transition from constant exercise in the outdoors to a sedentary lifestyle full of pressures and worries can be extremely difficult to navigate.

And he thought of the great mountains. A longing caressed him, and it was so sharp that he wanted to cry to get it out of his breast. . . . He covered his eyes with his crossed arms and lay there a long time, and he was full of a nameless sorrow.

—John Steinbeck, *The Red Pony*

IN MY CANADIAN hotel room, the film *Adaptation* played on the television. It was a movie I liked but had seen several times before and so it mostly existed as background noise. At one instance, however, Meryl Streep delivers a monologue that caught my attention and I paused to listen. "Most people yearn for something exceptional," she spoke. "Something so inspiring that they'd want to risk everything for that passion but few would act on it." She continued, "There are too many ideas and things and people, too many directions to go. The reason it matters to care passionately about something is that it whittles the world down to a more manageable size."

The Pacific Crest Trail had served that purpose for me. For two years it had been the biggest concern in my life. I researched the trail and read hikers' journals. I went on training hikes each weekend throughout the entire winter and spring leading up to my departure for Campo. Then for 132 days I lived it. I experienced everything I had so passionately dreamed about and was fortunate enough to maintain that passion through to the end.

I had whittled the world down to encompass only the PCT. There were too many things in my life I felt unhappy about and my single-minded devotion to the trail allowed me to shield myself from any anxiety about the trajectory of my life. I found the notion of the PCT so inspiring that I quit my job, moved out of my apartment, and put all my possessions in a tiny storage unit. There are too many directions to go in life when you aren't happy, haven't found what you're looking for, and don't even know what you want in the first place. So, I simply picked one direction—north, toward Canada. The only problem was that eventually I would reach the end of the trail.

So I did not walk into Canada a transformed and improved version of myself. I stepped off the trail as the same person I was when I departed Campo, with all the same challenges and problems waiting for me back in Seattle. I didn't go out there in search of anything profound. I hiked the trail because quite simply it seemed like too much fun to pass up. Too much beauty. Too much freedom. I suppose it's an impressive feat to walk 2,659 miles in a single summer, but these days there's nothing particularly unique about it. Thousands had done it before me and thousands more will do it after me. What matters most is the beauty I experienced, in all its various forms. The people I met and those quiet, calm, and serene moments when I was able to exist completely in the present.

It has been written of John Steinbeck that to him "truth was the product of poetry, and the kind of poetry that produced truth was the kind that came out of a close and inspired observation of life." On the PCT I was able to live a simple life, traveling through the country slowly by foot and carefully observing my surroundings. I hope in the pages of this book I was able to capture some of the beauty and inspiration I found out there in the mountains. I hope that I may have added a verse to the poem that is the Pacific Crest Trail. But then, as Steinbeck writes at the beginning of *Cannery Row*, "How can the poem and the stink and the grating noise— the quality of light, the tone, the habit, the nostalgia and the dream—be set down alive?"

Index

Note: Page numbers in *italic* refer to illustrations.

Acknowledgments

I WOULD LIKE TO THANK: my editor Jen Worick for her guidance and for believing in this book from the beginning; production editor Jill Saginario for expertly shepherding this book through the publishing process; art director Anna Goldstein for her guidance; Heda Padgen for her thoughtful copyediting; everyone at Sasquatch Books for giving me this opportunity and for bringing this book into existence; Jack Haskel at the PCTA for the information he provided and for tolerating my many questions; Barney Mann, a thru-hiker and trail angel who I did not get to meet during my thru-hike, but who took the time to share with me info about PCT trail markers and Forest Service trail signage; James Lewis and Eben Lehman at the Forest History Society for information about Forest Service logos and signs; Forest Service historian Lincoln Bramwell who directed me to info about "Bus" Carrell; Lisa Josephs, archivist at the National Steinbeck Center, for her thoughtful suggestions; Valia Pavlou for her help with bird feather identification; Erik for his friendship and bringing me a breakfast of honey buns and beer at Bird Spring Pass; my mother for her constant support during my thru-hike; and my wife Laura: the PCT connected us the very first time we met and you offered me immense support and encouragement during the entire creation of this book.

About the Author

JOSHUA M. POWELL grew up in Virginia, but during a cross-country road trip fell in love with the West. After two years working in Japan he settled in Washington State. He is an award-winning book designer and has also worked as a bookseller and a printing press operator. After a decade in the Seattle area he now lives on the opposite side of the Cascades with his wife in Spokane. Finding himself closer to the Rockies, he can't help but dream about hiking the Continental Divide Trail or Pacific Northwest Trail.